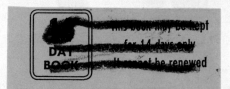

I Will Try

.

I WILL TRY

Legson Kayira

DOUBLEDAY & COMPANY, INC., GARDEN CITY, N.Y.

1965

To my mother with love for re-accepting me
after I had been fished out of Didimu;
to William and Martha Atwood with respect and appreciation;
and to Malawi
with a prayer for a happy future.

Contents

I

My Life in Africa

CHAPTER I

My Early Days

Sometime during the middle thirties a young man by the name of Timothy Mwenekanyonyo Mwamalopa Arinani Chikowoka Kayira went to live with his mother's people in a little village called Mpale in the hills of the Karonga District in the northern part of Nyasaland. Not too long before, the young man had lost his father, and a short time after the death of his father, his mother too.

Timothy was never taught the art of writing or reading or any worthwhile trade, but he was a hard worker. His mother's people, whose name is Kanyimbo, were kind people. They were neither rich nor poor, but they usually had enough to eat, and enough left over to feed an extra stomach. So they took the young man in. By the end of the thirties or the beginning of the forties Timothy was old enough to get married and take care of himself. He met a young woman whose family had just settled in the village. Her name was Ziya Nyakawonga, and her family was on the same social level as that of the Kanyimbos.

According to the custom better known as lobora a person who wants to marry has to give so many cows to the parents of the girl he intends to marry. Now here was Timothy with neither cows nor money with which to buy the cows so he could get married. His mother's people had cows, but they too had sons who would be getting married. But they were kind people. They gave him ten cows and he got married. That same young man, Timothy, and that same young woman, Ziya, became my parents.

Although my father was now married, he had not yet paid his in-laws all the cows, and I remember that even at the time when I was already a big boy, my mother's folk used to ask him for the remaining cows and threaten to sue him if he did not pay up. But he never gave them to them for the simple reason that he did not have any and had no way of getting any. He was a poor man. Gossip had it that so poor a man was he that in his whole lifetime he paid his poll tax only once. The headman of the village, seeing that my father could hardly find money for tax, declared to the tax collector that he was dead, and thus he saved him tax for the rest of his life. To the tax collector and to the Government he was dead, but to us he was still living. However, this peculiar exemption from tax did not put my father at ease. Indeed, it put him in a great difficulty, for it gave him the task of avoiding the tax collector, who had the nasty habit of making surprise visits into the villages.

I do not have the slightest idea when I was born. Either it was at the end of the thirties or the beginning of the forties. I do not know. But I know this: I was born, and that is what counts. To a Westerner it sounds strange that one should not know when he was born. To him it is insufficient just to know that he was born; he knows down to the last second just when it was. My parents, being illiterate, never knew how old they were. I can only say that since I was born, it follows that I was born during one of the twelve months and one of the days of the year, and each year as I ride the planet, drifting on its highway around, I pass my time-indicator registering how many times I have thus gone around, but I never know I am passing it, and have no way of knowing. Lucky is the horse, then, for his teeth tell his physician how old he is, while mine remain mute. I remember much later, when I grew up, I asked my mother if she could give me some clue as to when I was born, telling me some major events that occurred at or around that time, events that I would be able to trace so I could have some idea about the year of my birth. She remembered only that I was born at night during the season when people harvest. This let me argue with myself whether it made any difference to be born in May or June, the months of harvest, but as to what date or what year I could not tell, for the season has many nights and all of them are alike and, moreover, people harvest every year.

I never can say that I saw the hut in which I was born, for being old and in very bad repair, it had been pulled down long before my mind was sensitive enough to record and store a picture of it. I have, however, seen the place on which it was built, a small round place not measuring seven feet in radius. It was built in a relatively small village about half a mile west of a small river called Didimu.

I understand I was big and fat as a child and too heavy for my mother, who had to carry me around on her back. Inexperienced in handling her first child, and a heavy one, she decided to get rid of me by throwing me into the waters of Didimu. She did, and marched home with a light back and apparently no sense of guilt or lack of self-respect anymore than a girl who today realizes that her relations with some boy have gone too far and decides to abandon the result to some home.

But for my mother it was a different story. No sooner had she gotten to the house than an elder woman, carrying in her hands a baby whom she had just fished out of the water, came running, screaming, shouting and cursing, announcing to the rest of the villagers the unheard of thing: woman threw away her baby! "Now look here, you stupid," the women in the village reprimanded my mother, pointing their fingers at her, "look here, Mwenekanyonyo gave your father ten cows, and then you throw away his baby. You . . ." After some beating from my father, and frightened of what would follow if she repeated the offense, my mother welcomed me back to her. On that day I was given the name of Didimu as my first name, commemorating the name of the river in which I was tossed.

Two or three years later I had a brother. His name was Tennyson, the only one in our family who had a foreign name right from the start. I remember, when he was about three years or so, a certain man by the name of Nyondo gave us a puppy. Since we had no cows ourselves and hence no way of getting milk to feed this little animal, Mr. Nyondo agreed to let us bring the puppy to his house every morning and every evening and there he would give us the milk or we would let it suck from its mommy. My brother liked the puppy and he never forgot once to take it. One day, he came home crying. He did not have the puppy and, as far as I can recall, I never really learned what had happened to it. About a week later my brother was ill, and one evening during that week he died.

My father, one of the people who strongly believed that witchcraft existed, was not slow to admit that Tennyson had been bewitched. His belief was quickly confirmed, he thought, by the fact that before Tennyson was buried a group of old men in the village, with some sharpened sticks and reeds, had cut open my dead brother's stomach in order to determine what really killed him. They found that the bile in his gall bladder was black. "Well," they said to one another, nodding their heads in agreement, with one corner of their mouths turned down. "This is it . . . black bile! Well, that's witchcraft."

It was only a matter of weeks after the death of my brother that I was struck down by a mild cold. My parents lost no time in carrying me to a medicine man who lived several miles away. They could have taken me to my grandfather, my mother's father, who was also a celebrated medicine man, but they feared that his medicine would not be very effective on one so close to him. The doctor they carried me to was fairly old, not so tall as my grandfather, who stood close to seven feet. He had a short beard scattered over his chin, and short curly hair, gray almost white, suggesting he had seen a good many harvests. Chewing some leaves, he listened patiently as my father explained his troubles to him. "You see, doctor," my father began, "I had two children, and one of them just died this last month. Now this one is ill, and I have brought him to you so you can give him some medicine."

The doctor looked at me and nodded his head two or three times, then looked at my father and said, "I see, you have done the right thing in bringing this boy here. If you had delayed for another two weeks he would have died too." I began to cry, for I was afraid to learn that I would possibly have died in two weeks time. "There is a bad man in your village," he added, very careful not to mention any name, "who is planning to kill all of you."

My father was frightened at these words and looked as if he had never been told before that someday he too would die. "Help me, sir, help me, please," he pleaded.

Although I was still young at that time, I can still see the whole scene in my mind, the doctor seated there, listening to the pleadings of my worried father. My father, whose frame at its straightest measured not quite five feet, was sitting on a stool. An old black cloth hanging over his left shoulder gave him the pose of a Roman senator, a frightened one. His hair, black and short, made him look like a boy when compared to the doctor's. His front teeth were filed and they had the shape of a V. On his chin was a long black goatlike beard, of which he was very proud.

"Well," the doctor paused, then sighed. "I shall give him medicine that will protect him from any witchcraft, but before I do, I will ask him to promise he will follow the conditions I shall give him along with the medicine. These conditions are important, very important. If he breaks them, the medicine will be useless."

My father exaggerated the doctor's statement by saying to me, "If you don't promise, you will die in two weeks." I hope I will not be condemned when I say that I feared death so much I would do anything I believed would "immunize" me. I therefore promised the doctor I would follow his almost impossible conditions. My parents and the doctor rejoiced at my promise and called me a good boy.

"My child," the doctor proceeded, "here are the conditions. You shall never eat any mushrooms, you shall never eat the meat of a buffalo, you shall never eat any food that shall have been prepared by some person not related to you. . . ." There were about a dozen of them. This, I thought, is one good way of telling someone to starve himself to death, but I had agreed I would obey these conditions. After making a good many cuts on my chest, back, elbows, and thighs, and wiping some black powder on them, the doctor spat on my bare belly and then on my face. Patting me on the shoulders, he said, "Now, if you follow these conditions, there will not be any witch in this area who will have wit enough to find and bewitch you." Then he let out a short giggle and added, "And you will live to be as old as I am, or older." He gave my father some roots and ordered him to have them buried near the door post in our house. This was supposed to ward off witches.

Later on he became our family doctor. We consulted him on every matter concerning our health, and on the several occasions he would visit our home we would give him the best possible treatment.

I have mentioned witchcraft not only because my father strongly believed in it, but also because it was a popular practice at the time, and still is, though it is not so pronounced as before. The witches were supposed to be bad people, people who could magically strike and kill a person at will, and they were the people we were supposed to fear and avoid. On the other hand were the medicine men, who were supposed to be good people, prophets inspired by divine forces to control the power of the witches or to get rid of them. These were the people we were supposed to respect and admire.

Around that year I had a sister and she was named Nthope, meaning that the one preceding her in time was dead. My father took too much to drinking, and whenever he was drunk, he and mother would fight. The funny thing is that my mother brewed the beer for him, and normally he would invite his friends and they would sit down and drink all day. It was a good omen on such a day because when they were all drunk they would amuse one another by singing or dancing and he would not fight. But when he was the only drunk person, I seldom went into the house. He would sing, or he would command, "Now do this, now that . . . no. . . ." My mother would get tired of his noise and ask him to be quiet for a change, and then they would be at each other. My mother, towering almost a foot higher than my father when they both stood straight, and with a frame much more impressive, would say, "I say, stop this."

"Are you kidding? Who do you think you are, commanding me, me," my father would ask, pointing his fingers at his chest. Indeed, during such times my father felt like a king in the village and nobody could order him around. I feared that if a tax collector ever appeared in the village at one of these times my father would order him to leave right away. In fact, at one occasion he and others, including my mother's uncle, the great Mgejo, were drinking. My father turned around and, looking at the baldheaded Mgejo, said, "My, your little eyes are just as ugly as your mother's."

Of course he had never seen Mgejo's mother, who had died long before my father was born. Mgejo jumped into the house for a hoe handle, but my father had wits left in him to propel him away before the angry old man returned.

When they were fighting, my mother usually would bite him. They both had filed front teeth, but mother's were not so sharp.

At times he would ask me to sit down in front of him. With a small pot of beer immediately in front of him, and a straw made of some kind of a grass in one hand, he would teach me to write the figure six. This evidently was the only figure he knew, for he kept on teaching it to me over and over. Sometimes he would invite me to have a little drink. "Not even a little bit? O sure, you will drink it," he would say if I refused his offer. "What will you do when I am dead?" he would ask. "You know, I will always be asking you for beer, and if you don't give me any, I shall kill all your children," he would say, with a wide smile revealing his beautiful V teeth, and with one hand playing with his beard. This killing of my children if I did not give him any beer when he was dead was a reference to a belief that some people had. They were supposed to place some pots of beer on the graves of their deceased relatives, and if they did not, a calamity would befall them.

There were many other boys in the village, and like most of them I wore no clothes except a piece of string tied around my waist and a piece of cloth about five inches long and about three inches wide hanging on the string on my front, thus hiding my nakedness. Many was the day when I would lose the cloth and run around the village with nothing on at all, and I was never ashamed.

My father, who could make very beautiful baskets, was sometimes able to sell them and get sufficient money to buy himself and mother a piece of cloth. Normally he would buy black, durable cotton fabrics and my parents would wear them for three or four years before the cloths were in such tatters that it was almost impossible to pin the pieces together. Then my father would begin worrying and, one way or another, would get a cloth for my mother.

Those who had cows were lucky because they could sell some of them and buy clothes, but my family was not that blessed. We never complained about our poverty, and, indeed, there was nobody to whom we could complain. I was always proud that we had enough to eat, that all the food we ate was ours, produced by our own labor in our own garden. We never begged for any food. If only my father had been taught some worthwhile trade, hard worker that he was, I am sure that we would never have been so poor. He could make baskets, but so could almost everyone else in the village, and very few people cared about buying baskets, because they could also make them. Anyway, I believe that there has to be poverty if there is to be wealth, because I believe that there is no society where all people are the richest. In fact, if such a society exists, there will still be some who will be richer than others although they are all rich, and those who are less rich than the others will correctly be designated as poor in that particular society.

At that time boys and girls in our areas started to school when they were in their teens. The boys who were still young and those who did not like to go to school were charged with taking care of the cows. Girls did not have to look after cows. You will recall that I said we did not have any cows in my family. My mother's brother, Fred Kawonga, was such a lazy fellow that he liked neither to go to school nor to look after his father's cows, the cows my father gave them when he married my mother. I was to look after them myself, and I liked doing so especially when my grandfather would tell me that when I grew up they would all be mine. They aren't yet.

Then all the boys in the village were sleeping in a barn, the same barn in which the cows slept. It was a big barn built of wood, and grass-thatched like the regular houses or huts in the villages. Inside this barn was a row of pillars set about three feet from one another, and this row of pillars divided the barn into two sections lengthwise, separating our sleeping place from that of the cattle. The cows' section was built in such a way that it was slightly sloping so that when the cows were tied to the pillars at night, their tails would be on the lower part of the floor. This was meant to let the cows' water flow out of the barn instead of into our sleeping place. This did not help much because although the cows were tied to the pillars, some would get loose and wander to our section, pass their water or dung on us, and sometimes eat our little pieces of cloth. Besides, they were awfully noisy at night: some would endlessly snore, others continuously chewed cud, and still others breathed so loud and so violent that we would sometimes scream, thinking a wild animal was outside.

The nights were cool, and to keep ourselves warm we had a fire. To be able to keep the fire burning, we, of course, needed firewoods. We made a law for ourselves that everybody would bring a firewood each evening. First offense was to prohibit the offender from sleeping near the fire that night, and a repeated offense was punishable by dismissal from the barn. The general view at that time was that it was immoral for a boy to sleep in the same house with his parents, and if one did, we used to laugh at him and call him all sorts of names. There were limits to this. We would not laugh at one or call one names if he was seriously ill and had to sleep with his parents.

Fights among boys were very common. Sometimes we even had competitions, and boys from one village would fight boys from other villages. I always enjoyed watching these fights, but I never liked fighting myself because I was always beaten. We would be forced by the older boys in the village to fight hard so our village would win, but I did not like to be forced to fight, and the best I could do was run away from home. But I could not keep on running away all the time, so I had to learn to fight too. Aside from those frequent fights, we were very happy. Many times we would play hide-and-seek or we would bury one another in the sand and see who stayed under the sand longest. Of course, we had no way of telling how long one of us stayed there because we had no watches. The winner was given a prize, and prizes varied from day to day. Only once did I stay under the sand longer than anyone else, and I was to be given a grand prize, a ride home on a cow's back instead of walking. This was a prize all right, but I was too small to jump on the cow's back without any help and the boys were not cooperative. If I stood on a higher place such as a stone or a stump I thought I would be able to jump on the cow's back as it passed by. This I did, and it worked beautifully, except that I jumped too high and landed on the other side of the cow. If it were a jumping contest, I probably would have won, considering how high I went. When I hit the ground, a small piece of wood about an inch long pierced my left leg and it is still there. I have never thought of having it removed. I guess I will let it stay.

One of the people I was very fond of was my grandfather, my mother's father. Tukwewe Kawonga was his name. (I do not remember my grandmother very well because she died when I was still very young.) He had once given me some medicine that he claimed would protect me against all snake bites except that of a black mamba. His conditions, unlike those of our family medicine man, were simple. I would not kill a snake, and I would not jump across a dead snake. One day, he suddenly picked up his belongings, including the cows, and moved to Deep Bay about a hundred miles away by road. The reason for his sudden move was simple too. His older and only brother was ill and was being moved into our village where his sister Nacaro Nyakawonga would look after him. My grandfather was a very impatient man and in a way very inflexible. Early in the century, when his brother Mgejo Kawonga and he were young men, they had a quarrel, a very heated one. They had come to blows and Tukwewe was thoroughly beaten. He had been knocked to the ground, and with his mouth and nose bleeding, he rose, spat blood, and shouted, "Now look at me, you big boy. Look at me." His brother, bemused by his victory, turned his head and grinned proudly at his young brother.

"Now," Tukwewe declared, "you and I shall never see each other until the Judgment Day." Saying this, he picked up his spear and his axe and went away. They never saw each other again, although Mgejo as late as the forties made many desperate attempts through some mediators to see if his brother would change his mind. Even now that Mgejo has been dead for some fourteen years, my grandfather cannot go to the place where the house in which his brother died was built because he believes that since that was the last place his brother had been in, his soul might still be lingering there. He cannot set foot there, let alone see his grave. So when he moved to Deep Bay, I had no cows to look after, but I still continued to go out into the fields so I could play with the other boys.

I must have been about seven then. My mother had a baby boy. He was named Kamuntu, meaning a small man. There were now three children in our family: my sister, Nthope, who was quite grown up by then, Kamuntu, and myself. But not very long after the birth of Kamuntu, my mother became very ill, so ill that we all lost hope she would ever recover. My father moved her, together with Nthope and the baby, to our doctor high up on a hill. I was left alone at home and I was given the first test of determining whether or not, and if so, how far I would obey the conditions of my doctor about not eating any food prepared by someone not related to me.

Our chief food is sima. Women soak corn in water for several days, then they grind it or pound it in a mortar, and then sieve it, and they get a very fine white flour. They cook it in an open fire, and what comes out is sima. Luckily enough, before my mother became ill, she had enough flour in the house. She left it there and I was able to prepare my food.

At this time I was sleeping in our house and not in the

barn. I was very much afraid of the dark, and a young girl, older than I, by the name of Kelena Kafunda, was asked to sleep with me in our house so she could keep me company.

It was during the beginning of the rain season, the time when we begin to work in our gardens. Since my parents were away, I would have to be responsible for seeing that our garden was hoed and planted in order to be sure of having something to eat the following year. My mother's cousins, there were quite a few of them in the village, promised they would help me in their spare time. Our garden was such a big thing, around twenty acres, that I could not imagine how I was ever going to manage. Every day I would work in it for some few hours and I would plant every piece of ground that I had hoed. At the end of each day's work I would go home, prepare something to eat, then go out to play with the other boys. Sometimes my father would come down and work in that garden all day, then go back to the hill.

This continued for several weeks until one Saturday morning when I went to work a wee bit later than usual. It was still fairly early: the sun had not yet risen, the wind was blowing very gently, and the leaves on the trees were dancing in a gentle rhythm to the music of the wind. The leaves on the grass, like the leaves on the trees, were shaking and dancing among themselves. The monkeys up on a hill, the hill facing the one where my ailing mother was staying, were quarreling or singing or just plain shouting, I do not know which.

I had been at my work for not more than half an hour, and now I was standing up and watching two birds chasing each other a short distance from me. I guess one was female and the other male. What an early time for lovers to be chasing each other! Above me the clouds, dark and thick, were moving slowly, dropping some of their waters as they crept toward their destination. I wondered to myself if it was going to rain that day, and I was thus wondering when I heard a faint sound coming from far away. I listened, then listened again, and heard the sound of a drum. I listened still more and heard that it was a drum dispatching the message of death.

At home we have different ways of drumming, and other than the meaningless sounds of drums played by children, most of these ways of drumming have their meanings. One way signifies death, another signifies the presence of danger such as a lion, and so on.

"I wonder who is dead," I said to myself as I lifted my hoe to resume my work. Then suddenly a thought struck me: "Who else is ill? Could it be my ailing mother?" I listened again, trying to detect from which direction the sound was coming, and it was certainly coming from the hill where my ailing mother was. I almost fainted. I threw away my hoe and stared at the ground for many minutes. "If my mother is dead," I thought as the first tears rolled slowly down my cheeks, "what will happen to Kamuntu?"

The sound was loud and clear now, and its message was becoming clearer to me. I looked up and saw beyond a small river (not Didimu) that lay between our garden and the village, a small boy running toward me as fast as his legs could carry him. I saw him go down into the river and up again on the other side of it. I saw him getting nearer and nearer until he came and stood before me. He looked at me, panting violently, trying to regain his breath. Then he said in a soft voice, "They are calling for you, come quickly."

Now I was certain that my mother was dead. I left my hoe and ran with him to the village. There I found several women and men at our house waiting for me, but they did not tell me anything about my mother. All they said was that they wanted me to go with them and see how she was. I suspected they knew she was dead but were hiding the fact from me. We walked, and I could hear the chattering of the monkeys on the other hill. "They are happy," I thought, "but I doubt if they would be happy if they too lost their mothers." As we approached the village I heard the voices of women weeping, and I followed the people I was with until we got to the house where mother was. The first person I saw was my mother. My little brother was dead.

Evidently my father had left the house at night and gone to some other medicine man in another village so he could get more medicine, for no sooner had we reached the house than he came down, roaring. He resembled even more a Roman senator, a barefoot one, with a spear in one hand, an axe resting on his right shoulder, and a bunch of roots in the other hand. He flung away the roots, the medicine, for they were useless now. Tears rolled down my cheeks as I stared at the sad face of my mother, sitting there and weeping over her child, the second to die.

She lay down, sobbing and pleading, "Oh God, I am already dying, why did you not let me die instead, and let my little child live." And she kept on pleading as though she expected God to say, "All right, woman, here is your child. He is going to live, and you are going to die right now." She was very thin, and certainly ill. My father was also much thinner than he was the last time I had seen him. My sister was all right, except that when they were taking my brother to the grave, she cried violently, apparently thinking they were throwing him away. I had to hold her with all my might, for she struggled and kicked, almost tearing herself apart.

I stayed there with them for about a week. When I returned home, I found that the rest of our garden had been hoed and planted with maize. The people in the village had worked on it as a token condolence. A month later my mother recovered and came back home.

There were no roads in our area at that time, and whenever a white man happened to be passing by, there would be scores of Africans carrying his luggage, and sometimes carrying him. Our chief had received word that a white

Government official would be visiting our area and the other parts of the district, and he picked out several men from the village to carry his loads. My father was among them.

The journey was long and tedious, and it took them a long time before they finally got to our village, as the white man and his carriers were going from village to village, spending a night in each. I had never seen a white person before, and when the day arrived when he was due in our village, hundreds of us stood beside the path, awaiting his arrival. I saw a line of tired men, my father included, all carrying on their shoulders or on their heads chairs, tables, a tent, boxes, and many other things. It looked as though the white man was moving to some other place.

Slowly they passed us with no words and no smile on their faces. Behind these men was a suntanned white couple. The man was walking elegantly, not seeming to care about his heavily burdened carriers. His wife was lying luxuriously on a stretcher held by four of the strongest men of the group. They passed us, and we followed them until we came to a river where I saw the white man, who did not like to wade across the river, jump up on the back of an African. I watched the bearer as he staggered across the river, and wondered what would happen if that man slipped and fell, dropping his burden. But he did not.

We followed them still farther to the place where the carriers had set up the tent. I saw the chief bringing a fat bull as a gift to the white man, and other people bringing eggs, chickens, onions, and other gifts. I wondered how really important he was that people would so willingly give him bulls and chickens and other precious things. My mother and others in the village had told us children that he owned the country, and the way they told us it sounded as though not only was he a ruler but also the creator of our country. Little did I know that he was a foreigner, an exploiter, a man using us and our land for his own advantage under the guise of protecting us. Protecting us against what? Against progress? I did not know that any of those tired black faces, sitting innocently there, had, with the right tools, the right of occupying the office that man and his wife held. Anyway, for the time being I was satisfied with the false belief that he was my master, my mother's master, and every other African's master.

The following morning, he and his carriers left our village and went to the next one. When my father and his friends got home, they told us about an incident that happened on the way. My father and three others were walking behind the white people, and, being tired and hungry, they sat down to rest. One of them was carrying a big fat cooked chicken for the whites. Since they were hungry he suggested to the others that they should steal a thigh and eat it. They did. My father, who probably enjoyed it more than the others, asked why not just eat it all. Because, he said, "we have eaten this thigh, and he is going to beat us because of that. If we eat it all, he is still going to beat us. Why, then, don't we eat it all, seeing that we are going to be beaten either way? And besides, that way he is going to beat us with our stomachs full." They all agreed with him, and they quietly enjoyed the whole chicken and then resumed their walking.

The poor white man and his wife were hungry and they sat down waiting for their food. The men arrived. "My food," the European demanded, extending his arm to his food carrier. He got his food, but no chicken. Before he could ask what had happened to it, his food carrier told him they had eaten it. "You poor little devils," the white fellow murmured, ordering them to lie down while he went to fetch his stick. They had a very nice beating on their bare buttocks. We laughed, hearing of four such big men as our fathers being beaten by one man, but we advised them not to do it again, "lest he shoot you!"

We were approaching the season of harvest. All the

gardens in the area were heavy with maize, and beside each one you could see a man or a woman or a whole family, sitting there patiently all day guarding their gardens against the intrusion of monkeys, who had the nasty habit of coming down the hills to steal maize. Nthope and I would sit beside our garden and scream when the monkeys came down. They would be frightened and would run back or sneak into somebody else's garden.

We enjoyed doing this. As for me, I felt somewhat proud to be able to guard a garden that I had worked so hard to prepare. One day as we were sitting down waiting for the monkeys, Nthope fainted. I did not know what to do. I ran to my mother's cousin, whose garden was next to ours, and begged her to come and help me. She carried my sister back to the village while I remained, in case the monkeys should come down. During the following three weeks my sister was sick some days and all right others. Then the fourth week she began a turn for the worse.

One Saturday morning my father left for the medicine man. I went to do my usual job, watching our garden. My mother stayed at home with my sister. I came home in the afternoon carrying a basket of green maize. I found my mother's aunt, Nacaro Nyakawonga, holding Nthope on her lap while my mother was sitting with her head supported by her right hand. I saw that she was worried and guessed that my sister had really turned for the worse. My mother handed me a plate of sima which Nacaro had brought her and which she was not able to eat. I sat down and began eating it.

Then I heard my sister cough, a sharp strong cough, and neither my mother nor her aunt nor myself could doubt that she was indeed struggling with death. Her eyes opened and her mouth was still open from the cough. My mother motioned me to leave the room. With a lump of sima in my mouth and another in my hand, I stepped out. I spat out the sima in my mouth and threw away the lump in my hand.

As I walked slowly toward a house belonging to one of my mother's cousins, I heard a sharp cry from our house, then another. The two women were crying. My sister was dead. Soon there was a big crowd of men and women, and already someone was beating the drum. My father came from the medicine man, carrying in one hand his spear, in the other the bunch of roots, and on his right shoulder, his axe. He flung away the roots as he came into the house, but this time he threw away his spear and his axe as well.

Although I was young, I could not fail to be struck by the similarities between the deaths of these two children. They died on a Saturday, except that one died in the morning and the other in the evening. They both died when my father was away begging for some medicine, and then, on each occasion, he had flung it away because it was too late.

Unable to understand, I walked aimlessly around the area. There was a big noise as the women wept. It being late in the evening, my sister was going to be buried the following morning. That night in a quiet anger I wondered why she died, and for that matter, why did three members of the family die? I could not answer the question and I exploded into a violent crying and cursing. Oh yes, I even cursed the Lord Himself. I had been told many times that there was God who was all good and all kind. "Is this what you call kindness?" I asked the empty space in front of me, pointing my finger at it as if I saw Him there. "Is this kindness, letting other people's children die?" But that empty space before me did not answer. "Tell me!" I finally shouted in extreme anger, and aroused the attention of the men sleeping in the same room with me.

"We all die," they comforted me. "Of course, some die sooner than others, but sooner or later, we all die."

I had known my sister much more than I had known either Tennyson or Kamuntu, and I just could not admit to myself that she was dead. "Perhaps," I wildly imagined, "God is going to be kind this time and bring her back to life before dawn." But at dawn she was as dead as yesterday.

When they were carrying her to be buried, I walked behind that multitude of women and men and could not help but think of the days when she and I played together. I remembered when she had cooked something for her doll, and when her doll would not eat she became angry, and we laughed at her. She became more angry. Like a carpenter who curses when he hits his finger with a hammer, or someone who beats his car because it will not start, she was so angry that she destroyed her doll and even set our house on fire. I remembered the time she saved me a good beating when I had refused to do something my father asked. He was ready to whip me and my sister came with a stone in hand to stone him if he whipped me. He didn't. Now she was dead, and in a few minutes she would all be buried.

CHAPTER 2

I Go to School

It was around 1946 when I first went to school. That same year, we had very late rains. We had waited for weeks and weeks for the coming of the rains, but there were none. The village headman announced that he had set aside a day when all the people in the village would gather together and ask our ancestors to send us rain. On that sunny morning of the appointed day all people in the village swept clean their houses and extinguished all the fire according to the custom that had been observed by our people for centuries when praying for rain. Then we all gathered, and the leading men in the village made fire by rubbing two sticks together. Drums were drummed, and we danced and cheered, while our leading men said their prayers. Immediately after that each family took some fire and rushed to their houses. Pretty soon we saw a dark cloud yonder on the horizon, and it slowly spread all over the sky. The lightning flashed and the thunder rolled and the mountains echoed back, and there was rain! It rained and poured until the rivers were flooding high. Was that rain a result of our prayers, or was it natural?

The following morning, when many were collecting their hoes and seeds to go to work in their gardens, I was joining the other boys going to school for the first time. There was a three year school run by the Church of Scotland about three miles away from home, and there men and women were taught the art of reading and writing and our language and also some elementary arithmetic such as addition and subtraction. There were many pupils but very few teachers, and it was decided that those who were going to school for the first time should have their classes in the afternoon, and the others in the morning. So I was placed in the afternoon classes. The school fee was not very high, six pennies per year, but it took my parents several months before they were able to sell enough groundnuts to give me this money.

At school we had no books, no paper, and no pencils, and we did our work either on the ground with our fingers, or on our thighs with a piece of grass or of wood. The teachers had blackboards on which they wrote the work we were supposed to do each day. At the end of the day we could go home and show our parents what we had done at school.

At that time pupils brought food to the teachers. This was done in turns, and I remember one time when it was my turn my mother was not home, and when I went to school without the food I was sent home. The next day I cooked some potatoes and put them in an old dirty basket. The other boys were laughing at my dirty basket as I carried it to school, but the teachers ate all the potatoes and never complained about the basket. Besides bringing food to them, pupils were expected to work in the teachers' gardens or do any other kind of work around their houses. They claimed that since they spent most of their time teaching at school, they had no time left to do their other jobs, and so each day they would send so many pupils to do such jobs.

On one occasion the teacher asked us to bring hoes to school the next day, and several of us brought hoes as requested, and there were many others who did not bring any. The teacher said that those who had brought hoes should give them to those who did not bring them, and that each person should be the overseer of the person to whom he gave the hoe. I gave mine to one of the biggest boys in the group and collected several sticks for myself. He was a hard worker, and he worked as hard as he was able to, but I was never satisfied with his work, and I kept on beating him as he was working until he worked no longer but simply sat down and cried.

Then the teacher announced that those who were working should give back the hoes to the owners and be their overseers. I was scared to death at the thought that the boy I had just been beating so much would now be my overseer. What would he do? Was he going to avenge himself? I saw him wipe away his tears and laugh aloud with joy. Well, he collected several sticks and before he was able to beat me I ran home and did not show up at school for three days.

It had been very unnecessary for me to beat him just because he did not work to my satisfaction. Indeed, I believe I did not beat him because he did not work as well as I wanted him to, but because I had power, the power that the teacher had vested in me as an overseer of someone else. Many people have lost their heads because of power, and I lost mine too.

Few of the boys in the village went to school. Most of them were taking care of the cattle and were therefore unable to find time to go to school. This presented a great problem for me, because I liked to play with these boys out in the fields or go out hunting with them instead of going to school. The school itself meant very little to me at that time, and I would have been most happy if there had been no school at all. The teachers, too, seemed like cruel people who could punish or whip when one was late or did not bring food to them, and this discouraged me very much. Although I had been at school for less than a year I was already tired of it, and I was planning to quit, but my parents insisted that I continue, not that they knew the value of school more than I did, but because they did not want to waste the sixpence they had paid for my school fees. With much reluctance I finished that school year.

The following year there were six of us from the village going to school and there were many others from the surrounding villages. Unfortunately, all six of us did not like going to school that year. We were simply forced by our folk. We were able, though, to leave our homes and say we were going to school while in reality we would stop somewhere on the way and play there all day until late in the afternoon, when we would return home and report we had gone to school. However, things were made difficult for us later on because at school we were given slates, and our parents now wanted us to prove to them each evening that we had gone to school by showing them what we had written at school. In other words, after writing whatever we were supposed to write at school, we would let the teacher mark our slates with his piece of chalk, and we would run home without erasing our slates to prove to them we had gone to school.

Then one day one of us had an amazing discovery. It was simple, but it worked for us.

"You know, fellows, our parents cannot read!" our discoverer observed.

"So?"

"So we can hide in the woods again and play," he said, "then toward the end of the afternoon, we can write whatever we please, and show it to them. They'll believe it."

"But where shall we get chalk to write like a teacher? You know we have to have our slates marked by him."

"I have that answered too," he said, producing a piece of an old and well burnt bone. "See how it writes?" It wrote exactly like a piece of white chalk.

Now we were able to hide in the woods all day and go home in the evening and still prove to them beyond doubt that we had gone to school. Somehow they found out that we were not going to school and they punished us. The punishment was not severe, but it was hard enough to teach us to be honest. We had cheated, and had cheated nobody but ourselves. Our folk were forcing us to go to school, not for their own sake, but for ours. They were trying to help us prepare for our future, a future that would probably be better than theirs had been. They had never been given an opportunity to go to school themselves, but they knew very well that the knowledge of reading and writing and the ability to use such knowledge made quite a difference between a person who possessed such a knowledge and the one who did not have it. They knew, therefore, that if there was any chance for their children to go to school, they would not let them miss it. Our punishment was that we were made to march around the village all day singing *Azungu nzeru apanga ndegi* (Clever Europeans make airplanes) as we marched, a guard behind us ready to strike if one of us did not keep pace with the others. We were not allowed to stop for food or drink during the long march, and by the time our punishment was over late in the evening, we unanimously promised we would never refuse to go to school again.

A rumor went around the village saying that I had been responsible for passing out the information to the parents that we were not going to school, but instead were hiding in the woods and playing, and this did not please the other boys. They decided to punish me, and their punishment was to beat me. When we went out into the woods the following Saturday, they attacked me, but fortunately a relative who had just returned from Burma, where he served during the Second World War, was cutting some trees nearby. He was a strong man, and a good many people in the village were afraid of him. He heard my crying and came running to my rescue, and when the boys saw him, they all ran away. In the evening they were caught and punished.

It was not too long before we were reconciled. We went to school together again. On Saturdays we would go hunting wild animals for meat together, and in the evening we would all sit in front of a fire listening to stories told by our grandmothers.

"Children," the grandmothers would call out, "do you see that head on the moon?"

"Yea," we would all yell out together.

"That is ———. She used to be our neighbor, but one day she worked on Sunday, and God punished her by sending her to the Moon," they would tell us.

"Too bad," we would say with awe.

Going to school that year was no longer a hard thing. We loved to go and enjoyed being at school, and we learned, still more, that if we did things that were pleasant to the teachers, we would no longer be punished or whipped, and we made it our duty to do so. However, there was one thing that made us act contrary to our commitments, and this affected all the male pupils in the school.

The headmaster decided that all male pupils were to build a road running from the school to the main road, which was being constructed about two miles away from the school itself. The road was to pass through a fairly thick forest, and we were to work on the road for over four hours a day and be in class for about two hours. We started the job, and each day we labored there diligently.

But one of the teachers, who was also the village headman, sympathized with our toils, and instead of asking the headmaster to cut down the number of hours that we were putting on building the road each day, he advised us to strike and go home. We were not familiar with strikes, and certainly we were neither ready nor organized for it, but we tried it and it worked very well. We were in class for two hours one morning, then he sent us to work on the road. He himself remained at school, and while we were on the road, we sent a delegation to him composed of two boys, asking him to come and inspect our work, but before he and the two boys came, we all ran away. When we returned to school the next morning, he never mentioned anything about the road or about what we had done the previous day, and from that day on we never worked on the road. That was an easy strike, but why did the headmaster abandon the whole project just after one strike? In fact, we did not want to discontinue building the road, we were merely asking him to cut down the number of working hours a day. If all strikes in the world ended like that, business would probably have collapsed already! However, we were happier that way than we would have been otherwise.

That school year was a period of happiness and unhappiness, of gratification and disappointments, but we went through it all right, and we were all happy when the summer holidays came. I spent my holiday at home, most of the time hunting wild pigs with older men in the village.

I remember late that summer on a sunny Sunday morning, several men and three of us boys, armed with spears and dogs, left the village and went hunting up in the hills. We hunted all day but did not see any wild animals. Late in the afternoon we saw wild pigs. These pigs are good meat, but often they are dangerous, as they charge at people when they are attacked. The dogs began chasing them, and we ran behind the dogs, and when the dogs were barking, the pigs stopped to fight the dogs, and we came nearer to spear them; and the pigs ran again, with the dogs following, and us following the dogs, until we were able to kill one of the pigs.

We hid the pig in a small river and ran after the others until we were many miles from where we had hidden the one killed. We were unable to kill another one, and being tired, we sat down and rested in an old deserted house. And there came a heavy rain, and it rained all evening, stopping only late at night. Rivers flooded high, and our river quietly swept our pig down the slopes on the side of the hill opposite the one facing our village and deposited it in someone's garden down in the valley.

The next morning, finding that our pig was gone, we followed the river all the way down to the valley and found the owner of the garden with his family busy trying to take the pig to their house. It was hard to convince them that the dead pig was really ours, because they hardly believed our story. We threatened them that whether they believed our story or not, we were still going to get back our pig. Realizing that they would never gain anything by arguing, they yielded, and being kind people, we gave them a chunk of meat, about twenty pounds, which was better than nothing.

That summer my mother's cousin and her family moved to our village from another village about a hundred miles away. Their son, Maynard Sinkonde, was as old as I was and became one of my greatest friends. From the day we met in 1948 we played together, went to school together, lived in the same room, and shared our happiness and disappointments until the day we parted after attending Livingstone Secondary School in 1958.

In the eyes of the many people who saw us together, we looked like brothers, and not just like plain brothers, but twin brothers. Actually we did not look much alike, but still there were many people who could not tell immediately who was Maynard and who was Didimu. I owe much to my friend, especially in education. He showed a special interest in mathematics, and this is something I was very weak in, especially during the first few years of school. I remember at one time the teacher, seeing that we were great friends, feared that I would spoil him.

The next school year found Maynard and me at another school, called Wenya, which was then a junior primary school, situated about eight miles away from our village. Each morning we walked to the school together, and each evening we walked back home. It was a hard and tedious walk, and we seldom liked it. It became even harder in winter or rainy season when sometimes the mornings would be very wet. By the time we got to school we were very wet, and sometimes it would rain while we were already at school, and rivers would flood and we would be unable to go back home, so we would have to sleep with other people in other villages. Besides, there were many times when we got to school late, and we were either flogged on our backs or punished, and there were many times when we went home before we were supposed to because we were tired, and we would be subject to the same beatings. Food was a major problem. We seldom carried lunch with us, and by the time we got home in the evenings we were starving.

Around this time my mother had twin babies, a girl and a boy. We named the girl Nthembwa and the boy Kapampa, meaning that the girl was older than the boy.

My years at school, especially the first few years, were probably the unhappiest in my school history. My family, being so poor, could hardly afford to give me things that most of my schoolmates were able to get from their parents. Maynard was slightly better off than I was. He had brothers and some relatives who in our society were considered well-to-do people, and these relatives could help him in a number of ways. The school fees were high at that school, and one year my school fees were paid in a rather unusual manner. Mr. Zelenje's cows had wandered into our garden and had trampled on some crops. My mother had run to report to Zelenje's wife and Zelenje's wife welcomed mother with a couple of fists. My mother had run to the court clerk to sue Mrs. Zelenje. A week later I had my school fees paid and my mother could be seen displaying her new cloth.

It was, I think, April. We were sitting in the classroom doing our arithmetic. I had wanted to go to the lavatory for a long time, but the teacher would not give me permission.

"May I go to the lavatory now, sir?" I would ask again.

"Not yet," he would say. "Finish your work first."

"I have finished now, sir," I was able to say at the end.

"Have you really? Begin the next page."

Without his permission I could not go, and when he finally gave me permission I really went. I jumped out of the room in time, but no sooner had I started running to the lavatory than I was already helping myself. By the time I got to the lavatory, I was ready to turn back and go to the classroom. But could I? It was raining that morning, and all I was wearing was a piece of an old blanket about a foot long and a foot wide given to me by a friend. It was all in a mess. I could have gone behind the lavatory and run home, eight miles away, in that condition, or I could have run down to the stream and dipped myself into the water, but I did neither.

Another boy coming from the other classroom came running, and when he saw my trail on the ground he made a hideous scream and the school was out. When all the pupils were about to gather around me in some kind of an amazement, I almost smiled as if to suggest that these things are common and can happen to any person, but I was utterly ashamed. I looked like a little bird in its nest on a rainy day. It trembles as though it is running short of breath.

"My God!" one teacher was able to gasp.

"Go wash yourself in the stream," my teacher commanded. I did.

I quit school because of this incident. I was the subject of talk at school that week. People started their conversation in my name. "Did you smell him that day?" or, "What do you think of . . . ?"

I quit school, and neither my father nor my mother would force me to go to school now. I was not going to go; no, not to that school.

One of my mother's cousins, Kantuwarya Kafunda, had two wives. One of his wives, Nyamukwasi, was pregnant, and while I was staying home after quitting the school I was allowed to sleep in her house so I could make fire for her at night. Kantuwarya himself went to sleep in his other wife's house. One night I was awakened by my mother.

"Get out," she said, "there is a snake in the house."

"Give me a stick and I will kill it," I said, not knowing very much what I was talking about.

"You don't kill snakes. Come on, let's get out."

I went into the other house and slept there. The next day I was interested to know that there had never been a snake in the house that night. They did not want me to see the stork deliver his package to Nyamukwasi. I noted down the birth, in case at some future time the boy should ask us when it was that he was welcomed into the world: May 13, 1952.

Before the end of May my father received a letter from the headmaster. He asked me to read it, and I told him that the headmaster wanted to see my father at school. Actually the letter said that my father was being sued for neglecting to send me back to school. In a week or so, he appeared before the court, a local court about three hundred yards away from the school. He was fined five shillings but he could not pay it. He was to be detained at court and work there until he was able to pay the fine. Our village headman loaned him five shillings and he was out of trouble. When he got home he raised hell on me. And that is how I was finally sent back to school.

But the following year I was stranded again. I could not pay the school fees. However, this time the headmaster promised father he would pay my fees and have father repay him by installments. This my father did.

My mother had a baby boy. We named him Zgora, meaning that those before him were twins.

Then came another problem. My father began to feel uneasy about my well-being. During his beer errands he would meet a good many people, his beer partners. These partners would whisper into his ears that if he let me go on with school, some people in the village would feel jealous and bewitch me. He had not, however, forgotten that only a short time back he was fined five shillings for neglecting to send me back to school, but he knew also that if I failed my examinations I would not be permitted to go back to school except maybe under extreme conditions, such as if there were not enough pupils to constitute a class. This was his chance, he thought.

One day he called me to him. Sitting on his stool he began thus: "I fear they are going to kill you, my son, because you are passing all your examinations. Do you know what you should do?"

"What?"

"I am telling you that you should go and fail your forth-coming examinations. Write all the useless things you can think of and never give the right answers, and that way you will fail and nobody will bother to think of you anymore."

"Oh sure, I will," I promised him.

My mother was completely disturbed about it, and she asked how he knew they, the witches, were haunting me because of my school work. I was not going to stick to my promise, because to me examinations were competitions, the only times when I could also expect to stand on top of all or the majority of the pupils. I could decide purposely to fail my examinations, but I would be laughed at by many. I could decide to pass them, and I could be admired by many. I was, I decided, going to pass them and be admired rather than ridiculed, and besides, I feared that everybody would not believe my failure.

Then came that irritating routine. My sister and brother, the twins, were ill. My parents took them to the medicine man, the same medicine man, and still strange to say, it was again during the time when we begin working in our gardens. This suggested right from the start that I would have to take care of the garden again as I had done several years back. I was much bigger and I could do it better and more efficiently, but I had to think of school too. Before, I was not at school and I had all the time one could need, but I was small. Now, I was big and strong, but I had no time. I was going to work on Saturdays and once or twice during the week days I was going to skip classes.

At school the headmaster announced we were going to build six houses at school for boys whose homes were more than six miles away from school so they could board there. This order affected me. In one week, we had all the six houses standing ready for occupation. The routine was that we would go home on Fridays to get more supplies and come back on Sunday night and board there.

This left me with no time at all to work in the garden, and when I came back home on Friday I had to think of preparing myself some flour to take to school on Sunday night. This was solved because my father's cousin's son, Neckson Mukwala, was going to get me flour from his mother. When I learned that it was getting later and later for the garden to be finished in time for the rains, I quit school for one week and worked in the garden, but I still did not finish it. Then one morning all the people who belonged to the African National Church, the Church my mother belonged to, picked up their hoes and came to our garden, and by noon of that day the whole garden was done and planted with maize.

I returned to school the following week. I was a few minutes late the first morning and had to sit in the very back row of the big room during the morning prayers.

"Let's pray," said the headmaster, and we all bowed down with our eyes closed. But some boys in the back row kept on whispering and laughing, and the headmaster opened his eyes stealthily to note the boys. The whole of the back row, he decided.

". . . and in Jesus' name, Amen," said the headmaster finally.

"Will the boys in the back row come forward, please," he commanded, and at the same time dispatched another boy to get some whips.

We were standing in front of the whole school and the whole school had already judged us mischievous for making noise during the prayers. The whips were brought in, and one by one the boys were being flogged. It was my turn to be flogged.

"May I explain something, sir, before I get whipped?" I asked with my right hand raised up before the presence of the holder of the ultimate authority on the school grounds.

"You may."

"You know, sir," I began in trembling voice, "you know, I opened my eyes during the prayer, and I did so because I heard these people talk and laugh, and I wanted to see who were talking and laughing so I could report them to you, sir, at the end of the ceremony."

"Very well," said the voice of one with authority. "Very well, go back to your seat."

I had gone about two steps when that same voice of one with authority, rang behind me.

"Wait a minute. You were not at school all last week, and do you have any explanation? I'm sure you do. Let's hear it."

I stood at attention, my hand raised up, and I began to explain. My family was not home and I was left with the job of hoeing the garden. "That's why, sir," I said.

My explanation, he said, was satisfactory, but I was still going to be whipped because I had not asked his permission to stay away.

The game we played most often at school was football, soccer, and in January 1953 my school went to play the Nthalire School, some twenty miles away. The whole school went up there to cheer the players and it was exciting to watch the two teams fight for their schools. Unfortunately we lost the game. It was expected, however, because whenever we played Nthalire at Nthalire, we lost the game, and whenever they played us at Wenya they always lost.

The next morning we started walking back home by way of my village. As we were approaching my village, we could hear the drum, that same old drum that tells you right away that someone somewhere is dead. I was not surprised when I found a number of people at home, getting ready to go to the place where my ailing sister and brother were. I went with them and found it was Zgora who was dead. Again I could not fail to recognize the similarities between the deaths of Kamuntu and Zgora. Whereas, Kamuntu died on Saturday morning, Zgora died on Saturday night. When Kamuntu died, my family was staying away because my mother was ill, and when Zgora died, my family was staying away because Nthembwa and Kapampa were ill. And on both occasions, I had been left alone to till the garden, only to be helped at the end by the villagers.

The following month I volunteered at school to go along with ten other boys to Bulambia, about seventy miles away, to get school supplies. I realized that it was going to be a rough hike, and that if my mother and father were home, they would never let me go, but I had never been up there before and I was eager to see it. Besides, that was the school where those pupils who had completed the school I was then attending went, and it was within the realm of possibility that I would go there too upon the completion of my schooling at Wenya. Also, there were two boys attending that school from my village and they were close friends of mine, and I was anxious to see them.

We carried our packs of corn meal and off we went. It took us fifteen hours of walking before we finally got there. We were given our bundles of books to carry back to our school, and mine was one of the lightest because I was the youngest of them all. It contained nine dozen textbooks, two dozen notebooks, one dozen rulers, and four slates. It was the heaviest load that I had ever carried on such a long trip, and it was not very strange that I was the slowest of them all. The trip took us more than fifteen hours to get back to our school. I stumbled on the way, dropped my bundle to the ground, and hurt one of my toes on the right foot. I picked up my load and I found that one slate was broken into numerous tiny pieces.

My toe hurt terribly, my load looked heavier than it really was, and I was extremely tired, too tired to walk something like a mile without stopping for a rest or two. There were times when the other boys would leave me about four or five miles behind, and they would stop and rest while waiting for me, and when I arrived they would start again. At times when they were thus waiting for me, one of the older boys would run back after me and carry my load to the place where the rest were resting. We got home late at night and I immediately forgot all my tiredness and pain when I learned that my brother and sister were well and that the family was back home.

I had always used Didimu as my first name, but while I was attending Wenya School, I noticed that most of my schoolmates had English sounding first names. Also at that time I was learning English, and I took quite a pride in the few words that I had mastered so far, and I always boasted that I would learn as much English as possible and so be able to speak it much better than those who were teaching me English. To satisfy my pride I decided to coin an English sounding name for myself. One other fact that prompted me to change my name was the fact that many people used to laugh at me. Didimu is also the name of Thomas, the doubting disciple, and so sometimes the other boys and girls referred to me simply as "one of the twelve," meaning, of course, one of the twelve disciples, and sometimes they referred to me as Mr. River, meaning the river in which I was tossed when I was a baby and from which I got the name of Didimu. My grandfather had given me the name of Chalangani, which means *useless* or *unintelligent*, and I hated this name because I believed I was not unintelligent, at least not as unintelligent as the name suggested.

One day when I was still thinking of getting myself an English sounding name, the name Legson came into my mind. I had never known anybody who had this name, and I do not know anybody who has it, and I cannot say exactly why I stuck to this name and not another.

Maynard, my friend, wrote on the walls of the houses in the village and elsewhere with a piece of chalk in big letters DIDIMU LERO NI LEGSON, that is to say, "Didimu becomes Legson." I announced that I would fight any boy or girl who called me Didimu, and I would be most pleased if all men and women in the village began calling me by the name of Legson. So my name was changed, but my father always called me by my old name, and once in a while some boys would forget and call me by the old name and this would result in fierce fighting. My brother and sister found it hard to pronounce my name and they have always called me by the name that sounds like Ligisoni.

Later on, when I began to understand very well the reasons why the British are in Nyasaland and what they are doing, I began to be more and more pleased if someone called me by my old name. I began to look upon anything English with some reserve. Didimu is the name, and the right name, for me. It is African in every respect, and it has all the meaning a reasonable name should possess. I was born a proud African and was given a proud African name, but because of the foolishness that sometimes befalls some men's minds, I was inclined to change it and give myself some foreign name that was void of any meaning. My father was very right to call me Didimu and refuse to call me Legson, and the very fact that my brother and sister found it hard to pronounce this foreign name indicates how really foreign it was, and who would care to keep such a name? Yes, it was indeed an error that I so rushingly demoted my dignified and historical name.

The following year, instead of going to school in Bulambia as was normally the case, we went to Nthalire, where the senior class had just been introduced. This senior class was supposed to be put at Wenya, but for some petty reasons and after opposition to our side, the class was put at Nthalire and so Nthalire automatically became a senior primary school while Wenya remained a junior primary school. There were no boarding houses at Nthalire, and so we lived with families and went home once every two weeks. The headmaster, Mr. Morton Mughogho, who is now a school inspector, was a very intelligent teacher, and we all liked him, although he often spanked us. During the first week of school he announced that he wanted every boy at school to be in khaki shorts and a khaki shirt, and all girls to be in blue dresses. This was much more than my family could afford, and I knew very well that no matter how I tried to tell the teacher about my situation, he would not very likely understand me, as he had no idea at all about my background.

All I was wearing at that time was an old piece of white cloth, which was so old and so dirty that it was no longer white and would never be white again no matter how much I washed it. As a matter of fact, it looked more like khaki than white, and the teacher at one time asked me if I could just make a shirt out of it. This would have been possible, but then I would have had no shorts to go with it and it would have been senseless to wear a shirt without shorts, and besides, I used it as a blanket at night. Once again I quit school for several weeks. One of these days when I was out of school and working in our garden, a man by the name of Eliah N'gambi, nicknamed Nairobi because he often talked about the days when he had worked in Nairobi, saw me and asked why I was not at school. He gave me a pair of khaki shorts and a white shirt and put me back at school again.

While at that school I was staying with a family about two hundred yards from the school grounds. I was able to go home at noon and have lunch. The teacher gave us nicknames, and mine was "girl" because he claimed that I looked like a girl. During the first three-week holiday I went to Karonga Boma, a town, and worked. The following year found us at Wenya again, that is, the senior class that was transferred to Wenya, so that although both Nthalire and Wenya were senior primary schools, Wenya was higher in that it had one class higher than Nthalire.

In summer of that year I had worked at various jobs. I

had worked at a dam, I had worked on the road, and I had worked in the gardens digging bands. The Agriculture Department demanded that people dig some sort of streams along or across their gardens. These streams were to be one foot deep and three feet wide, and were to collect the running water after the rains which otherwise would sweep away the soil. Owners of the gardens paid me for that. Then one day, late that summer, some men in the village were going to sell their cattle in the southernmost tip of Tanganyika, and they needed some boys or men who would help take care of the cattle on the way to that place and then carry things they would buy there back to the village. This was a long journey and they estimated it would take three to four weeks to get there and about a week to get back. My father had thought of going with them, but he changed his mind because he was in the act of building a house, and moreover, my mother had had twins, one of whom was already dead, and the other, who was given the name of Masida meaning that they were born two but the other one is dead, was herself in poor health. I was to go with them instead. There were nine of us in all, and two of us, Diaford Nyirongo and myself, were to take charge of the sixteen cows on the way. On a Monday morning my father bade me farewell.

We had been gone a week, when I remember one morning I woke up crying. It had been a cool night, and we had slept outdoors, not very near any village. Once at night the other men had waked me, saying that I was crying. I said I was not crying. I went back to sleep and got up crying. I had had a bad dream. I dreamed that my head had been shaved and that I had been crying in protest against the shaving of my head, when suddenly I had seen in my dream a lone man standing in front of me with his face turned away from me. I recognized this lone man to be my father.

It was on Sunday, the Sunday following the Monday

we left home, that my father, after a good drink of beer, went out into the woods to get himself some construction material. Away into the bush, far away from home, we were ascending and descending hills, and away in the woods my father was climbing a tree, higher and higher he went until he could go no higher. He cut down some branches and after dropping his axe, he began climbing down, but he had stepped on a dry branch which immediately broke, bringing him down with it. He fell on his branches, breaking his hand, a compound fracture. His other hand landed on the axe and was badly cut, and his head hit a rock and cracked. Heaven knows how long he stayed there unconscious. But he regained his consciousness and staggered home, sobbing and crying as he staggered. He got home and was carried to a dispensary eight miles away. He lived three days, then died.

The men had sold their cows and they paid us eight shillings a piece. With this money I bought myself a blanket. I thought my mother and father would be very proud to see me be the first member of the family to own a blanket, but only a grave of father did I find.

I started a new garden not too far from our house. By the way, the house my father was building before he died, was never completed. I had asked some friends to help me to do it because I was running short on time as the schools would be starting soon. I had climbed a tree to cut down some branches, and I narrowly escaped being knocked down by one of the branches as it came down. I came down too, and the other boys thought it would be a good idea if we did not climb trees.

I was cutting down one tree while standing on the ground, and as I swung the axe, some little branch deflected it and it came right on my right leg. I had cut myself, and I saw blood rushing out. I tied a string around my thigh so I would not lose much blood and slowly walked home and one of the boys ran home to report my accident. A group of men, women, and children came running to carry me home. My friend had exaggerated when telling them of my injuries, for upon hearing the report they thought I was in as bad a condition as my father when he fell off the tree. And that is the reason why the men and the women came to carry me home. My mother was weeping already before she saw me. I was taken to the same dispensary where my father had stayed during the last three days of his life. Only I did not stay there.

I had not seen him when he lay in that dispensary after his accident, but from what I had heard, I knew that I was not even half as seriously injured as he had been, but my mother, who had seen my father in that condition and who saw me then, had a different idea. He fell off a tree, hurt himself and died, she reasoned. I cut myself while felling a tree, therefore she concluded I was going to die. She hurried to a medicine man and asked his advice.

"This is a simple case," he told her. "You see, his father and all his relatives now dead are sad because they think he is being troubled, so they want to free him of these troubles by letting him die."

She came back more worried than she was before she went to him, for now she even blamed herself for having ever gone to consult him in the first place, because, she reasoned, she would have felt better if she did not know my fate. She even wished the doctor was not telling the truth. He had suggested to her that one remedy to this was that we should move from the area to some other place.

I did not stay at the dispensary for long. I came home, and one more thing that still shook my mother and this time, it shook me too, was an incident a short time after my accident. I was sleeping on the same mat with a nephew of hers. Chapimba was his name. We were both covered with the same blanket, and it happened that late at night there was a snake between us. As far as I can recollect now, it appears that my friend shook first and got bit on the back. Not knowing what had happened, he went out and sat on the verandah crying. When his mother heard him, she came out and asked him why he was crying. He could not tell. I heard them talking outside and I went out, leaving the blanket on the mat. Light was brought to check if there was anything there, because it had been noticed that his back was swelling. A little black snake was lying on the mat under the blanket. It had bitten him, and at that hour of the night there was little they could do in terms of medicines. The little they did, did not help the matter, for it was not too long thereafter that our friend died.

Our doctor suggested that we should move to another area, because he said there the spirit of any of my dead relatives would not find me. I was in my senior class and soon I would be going to a secondary school, and secondary schools were far away. My mother was planning to move to some other area too, but I found it useless to run away because I said, "If the spirits of my dead relatives are trying to haunt me, I cannot escape them by running away."

"You don't understand," responded my mother. "Let's get out of this place while we have time."

"And what's it that I don't understand?"

"What the doctor is telling us. He says we are all going to die if we don't move soon."

I was not going to move because he told me so, I said. She was getting angry, and she began packing. "Why do you insist on staying here?" she asked.

"But where are you going?" I asked. "You have a house here, a garden here, you have friends here, and now wherever it is that you are going, who do you think will build you a house, who do you think will begin a new garden for you?"

"I don't care. I don't care at all," she answered.

"You better care. You will not have a garden, and you will not have any food, and you will starve to death, and that will be the death your doctor is predicting."

She cooled down and unpacked her things. We stayed there in our good old village, and we enjoyed our stay there as much as we could, much more than we would had we decided to move.

"Do you still want to move away?" I asked her two years later.

"Oh, yes. I certainly want to move away," she replied. "But I just do not know where to."

"Is it not madness to run away from your good home because a witch doctor tells you to?" I asked.

"It is indeed madness to stay there when he tells you to go," she said.

"That may be true," I said. "But let us stay here a little longer. I am sure it will be all right."

I sat for my final examinations that year and I passed them. I had applied to a teachers college but was turned down because they said I was too young to be a teacher. I applied for a bursary, or scholarship, from my district and they granted me five pounds for my school fees at a secondary school, but that was not enough. Maynard got help from his cousin who was then a teacher, and he was going to a secondary school. I just could not help thinking that I would have to loaf in the village because I could go neither to a teachers college because I was young, nor to a secondary school because I did not have enough money. But, then, I had a very rare chance, a rare good fortune which Providence gives to few people in a long time. I received a letter from an Englishman named Petty, a missionary at Livingstonia Church of Scotland, an old and famous mission school in the country founded by Dr. Robert Laws during the latter part of the last century and named after the Scottish explorer, none other than David Livingstone, who traveled far and wide into the heart of Africa, exploring and pioneering for the abolition of the slave trade.

It was in 1859 that the weary missionary, after a great deal of traveling, set foot in the southern part of what is now Nyasaland, thereby discovering Lake Nyasa. A little over a decade thereafter, Dr. Laws appeared in the country and established the mission school in the northern part of Nyasaland and named it after that famous missionary. The school started in poor buildings, with only a few students, but in time Dr. Laws, with his untiring efforts, built new beautiful modern brick and stone buildings, which still retain much of their beauty and modernness. Many years after Dr. Laws's death, the school developed into a secondary school, and the Reverend Petty was living at that school although he was entrusted with the affairs of the schools in the Karonga District whose headquarters was Livingstonia.

I had seen him several times when he visited our school, but I had never been introduced to him, and really there was no reason why I should have been so privileged, so he did not know me, but I knew him. Only three years before, he had been instrumental in introducing standard four at Nthalire school instead of at Wenya, thus making Nthalire a senior school. Because of this, many of us in Wenya looked to him with some indifference because we were never satisfied with the reasons why he and others had done so. But that year this man we had been indifferent to was doing a favor for me, my village and my area, and possibly my country.

After the final examinations Mr. Petty, being in charge of the schools in my district, had a copy of the list of the names of those people who had passed, and when he saw my name high up on the list, he inquired what my plans were. The people he asked, happening to know much about me, replied that I would be able neither to join the teachers college because I was too young nor to enter a secondary school because of my financial incapability. Losing no time he mailed a letter to me with a stamped and self-addressed envelope enclosed for my reply.

I was very excited when I received the letter because at that time I was not used to receiving any and it was one of the few that I had received in my whole life. Actually I had written and read many letters, not my letters, but letters belonging to those people who could neither read nor write. When such people received letters from their friends or relatives working or living in distant places, I was called upon to read them for them, and whenever they wanted to write letters to their friends I was asked to write them. Taking a pencil and paper, I would write down what they dictated to me as though I were their secretary. But this letter was different. It was mine!

I opened it with trembling fingers, wondering where it came from and what message it carried. I spread it open and began reading. "Dear Legson," it began, "You have passed your examination with high marks, and I understand you do not have money to go to a secondary school. I talked to Mr. Russell (headmaster) of Livingstonia Secondary School, and when he saw your marks, he immediately agreed to reserve a place for you here. . . . I shall help you through secondary school so that you in turn will help someone." I read the letter over and over again, and I was filled with joy.

CHAPTER 3

Livingstonia

WORD passed round in the village that I was going to a secondary school. Few congratulated me, and some went as far as commenting, "There is no end in learning. Why don't you just quit school now and get yourself a job and earn some money? You don't know when you will die; you might just keep on going to school and die without even making use of your learning." Others commented privately. "Do you know," they asked one another, "Legson is going to a secondary school? Legson and his friend (Maynard). Just imagine! They are very proud now, and how much more proud will they be when they come back. We won't even talk to them."

As for mother, this was nothing to be very excited about. As for me, it was just wonderful. I reflected on my life and saw a boy born of a poor family, marching on the road of poverty, the road on which thousands of millions of people had marched before me, and many more will march after me, but I saw myself as one of the very few fortunate ones of those millions of poor people, for although I was poor, I was permitted to go to school, and, what is more, I was even promised help to go to a higher school. Other poor people such as my parents were not even lucky enough to attend the very first grade, not even to learn to write their own names, let alone counting further than twenty.

But here I was, having been in school for over nine years

and not yet satisfied with the little education I had so far acquired. Therefore I would not lose such a great opportunity, the opportunity that happens to one sometimes only once. Mother would have been pleased to see me employed. Since my father had died the family was, in a way, depending on me. I explained to her that if I went to a secondary school and got through all right, I would have a better chance of being employed, and not only that but that I would also be in a better position of finding a better job with better pay.

But to her it made no difference. Any job was like another and it did not matter which one I took. However, she was soft, and acting under pressure from those few people who understood what it meant to go for higher education, she let me accept Mr. Petty's help. Wasting no time, I hurried and borrowed an ink pen from a neighbor, and, tearing a piece of white paper from an old notebook, I wrote to Mr. Petty, thanking him for his great kindness, and assuring him that after my secondary school and when I got employed, I would do all in my power to help one or more who were in need.

Three days later I received another letter, this time from Mr. Russell, the headmaster of the school, admitting me.

The school was about two hundred miles from our village, and both of us, Maynard and I, were to go there by bus. The mission, aside from operating the secondary and elementary classes, offered several other departments such as engineering and carpentry, teachers' training, theological training, and medical training.

Because of these various departments, several people in our village had gone there to receive one kind of training or another, and most of these people used to walk there. They had often told us about their troubles on the way, and also about the mission. One thing that they all agreed on, and which they all liked to talk about most, was that the place was very cold, and that it rained a great deal more and much more often than it did at home. Mr. Russell, too, in his letter had emphasized the same point, and he asked me and all other incoming students to bring raincoats as well as plates, forks, spoons, flashlights, and so on. But both Maynard and I were anxious to go and see for ourselves this famous institution of learning.

We made all the necessary arrangements. Maynard bought himself a pair of canvas shoes, blankets, and a pair of short trousers. I still had my old blanket, the blanket I bought in Tanganyika when we went to sell cows, the same blanket that gave me the distinction of being the first member in our family ever to own a blanket. It was now old and no longer attractive, but I was still proud of it. I had bought it with my own money earned by my own labor and toil, and certainly it was worth being proud of.

Mr. Harrison Kayira, my teacher at Wenya, gave me a pair of short trousers and twenty shillings for my bus fare to the school, and Mr. Kamalenje Kanyimbo, my father's cousin, who also had helped me in a number of ways before, gave me a white shirt. My mother prepared some corn flour and killed a chicken for my food on the way. We were going to walk from the village to Polomombo, a day's journey, then catch the bus to Mpachi and walk from there to the school, a distance of eighteen-odd miles.

On the great day for our leaving, we washed ourselves and ate the food that our mothers had prepared for us. Then came the moment for our goodbyes. We were going to miss our families for three months and then see them for three weeks if we were able to make it. My mother was sad to see me off, and she began giving me her last advice, the same things she had been telling me all of the past week. "Now, my son," she began, "you are going to a strange place, and you don't know anybody there. When you get there, don't fight with the other boys, don't quarrel, be kind to others, help them and they will help you, and remember to write us, and leave all the girls alone."

About a year before that, her cousin's son had died and it was believed that he had gotten a disease from some woman when he was teaching in another district. This was what led my mother to say, "Leave all the girls alone."

"Do you understand?" she asked.

"I surely do," I replied.

"Do not think this is a joke," she began again. "I am serious. If you fight, they will kill you. If you are kind to them, they will be kind to you; if you are friendly they will be friendly to you; if you are mean to them they will also be mean to you; and you know why your friend died."

"I know all that," I interrupted her before she mentioned girls again. "I know all that," I repeated.

"Yes," she continued, "you better know all this. I am doing this for your own safety and happiness. I am not the one who is going to suffer, you are the one who is going to suffer when you will have no friends, or when no one will help you."

"Mother," I said, "certainly I know all that, and do not worry about me. I shall remember all that you are telling me now. What else do you want me to remember?"

"Just remember what I have told you. If you . . ." She began to say them over again, and I was getting tired of them and was already angry.

"Well, if there is nothing else you want to add," I told her, "then goodbye." I picked up my things, and Maynard, who was also being told the same things, was ready, and off we went, and my mother still was shouting, "Don't forget."

It was a long walk, and there was only one village between ours and the village where we were going to catch the bus. We hurried forward, now walking, now running, until we came to the in-between village around eleven in the morning, but we still had a long way to go. Through tall trees and tall grass, we passed. The sun set, the darkness spread, and we were still walking. It was around eleven at night when we finally reached our destination. The villagers welcomed us, and they said that we were very lucky that we did not meet any lions on the way. "Just yesterday," one told us, "a lion was killed nearby, and today two lions were seen here. You are very lucky, my boys, but please never travel at nighttime in this part of the country, and don't be out of doors at night." Late in the evening the following day, our bus arrived and took us to Rumpi. Neither of us had been in a bus before and we were very anxious to ride one, although we were a little bit afraid, afraid of the bus because we feared it would crash anytime, or, worse still, miss the bridges, in which case we would end up in the rivers. But the bus safely brought us to Rumpi, then to Mpachi, from where we walked to Livingstonia.

The pair of shorts that Mr. Kayira had given me were too big for my waist, and I feared that it would cost me a great deal of money if I sent them to a tailor and have him change them. An idea popped into my head, "Why not buy a belt?" Long before the school opened I went to the stores. To my disappointment most of the belts I found there were very expensive. As a last resort I looked around at the ladies' belts and saw a cheap green belt. If it can do the job as well as any other belt can, I thought to myself, I am buying it, and, sure enough, I bought it and wore it right there in the store and proudly marched out with a lady's belt around my waist, and whom did I meet outside? Mr. Petty! I introduced myself. "My name is Legson," I began.

"Oh, how are you?" was the response.

"I am very fine, thank you."

"How old are you?" he asked.

He was speaking too fast for me and I missed the word "old" and thought he said, "How are you?" again. I wondered why he asked me the same question twice. So I answered again, "I am very fine, thank you."

"Thank you," he said, "and how old are you?"

Now I understood him. "I don't know how old I am, but I think I am fourteen," I said.

"I will put you in school at nine," he said.

The school was opening at nine o'clock that morning, and I rushed to the dormitories so I could get ready. We had arrived there at night and I had not seen all the students, but now in daylight I saw that they were many. One thing came into my head immediately, "What will these people think of my lady's belt?" And worse still, I noticed that over three quarters of them had shoes on, and that I and the others were walking around barefooted. Nobody laughed at me for the time being and we quietly went to the opening ceremony.

Afterward we, the newcomers, gathered in one big room, which was to be our classroom for that year. Mr. Russell came in to give us the textbooks, pencils, and so on. He had a list of our names, which were arranged alphabetically, and the numbers we got were to be our numbers for that year. He mentioned that if he called out one's name, he would give that particular person his number and the textbooks. It happened I was number six, and the people whose numbers ranged from one through five were absent. He called out my name, and I did not hear him. He called out again, and I still did not hear him, and yet again he called out, looking at me as he called out my name, and I was still looking at an old book I had brought with me from home. I looked up at him and he looked at me. "What is your name?" he asked.

"My name is Legson Kayira," I answered.

"Then why don't you answer when I am calling?"

"I didn't hear, sir."

What a poor impression, I thought to myself later on. Maybe he thinks I am nuts! Later on that afternoon we were measured for our uniforms, but it was over two months later when we finally had them. After the uniform measuring period, we were given the rest of the afternoon to roam around and discover the place. We were much impressed with the school buildings and all other buildings there. I had been very puzzled all that day about the many telephone wires I saw there, and I asked a fellow if he could explain to me why they had so many telephone wires. He laughed, finding that there was someone going to a secondary school who was not yet familiar with electricity, and added, "These are not telephone wires, they are electric wires."

It was not long before we discovered that the place was really cold. With only one blanket I found the nights even cooler. Our beds were made of bricks with a cement top, so both the nights and the beds were cool. I bought myself a mat, and every morning I could make my bed simply by spreading my mat on the bed and then spreading the blanket on the mat, and every night I slept between the mat and the blanket.

Cold was not the only problem. For several weeks I found it very hard to wash my only pair of clothes, and later on a Mr. Changala, who was a senior student there, used to lend me his jacket whenever I washed my things, and at such times I could wear a jacket without any underwear inside. Still later on, another senior student, a Mr. Nyondo, had been inquiring about my background. When he learned that my father was dead and that I was partly depending upon my mother and partly upon myself, he wrote a letter, which was delivered to me by another senior boy. "Excuse me for conducting an investigation of your background without your consent . . . and considering your situation I have wondered if I can be of any assistance to you. I have a white silk shirt, and I shall be more than happy to give it to you if you want it." I accepted the shirt.

We were buying our own soap for washing, and there were many boys who were more than willing to share their soap with me.

One of my favorite days at Livingstonia was Sunday. I enjoyed going to the Sunday School as much as I had enjoyed it while still home. I enjoyed hearing the organ play on special Sundays, and if I could have been in a position to decide which hymns to sing, we would probably have been singing only "Rock of Ages." I liked it.

In our Sunday School class, I was very much taken by the good looks of a young girl. Her name was Emma Munthali, and she came from Mlowe. Oh yes, I saw in her what I thought of as the model of a beautiful woman: short, with a fairly short forehead and sharp brown eyes. But she had a boy friend, a Mr. Chilufya from Northern Rhodesia. Moreover, she was older than I was, although she was three years behind me academically.

I had courage to write her a letter, and sure enough she wrote me back. My first letter from a girl! I felt like I was not walking on the same ground that we all stood on, but was only bouncing in the air. I felt as though she had already agreed to marry me, and as if we had already set a date when we could get married. But I had never talked to her, except through that first letter, and in the letter I had not once mentioned anything about what I thought of her. I had to worry about her boy friend. I was not going to let him know I was after his girl.

To my joy her parents told him he could not marry her because his home was far away in Northern Rhodesia. Well, my home was only a little over two hundred miles away from hers, and this would not be a deterrent. I wrote her, and this time I told her what I thought of her. Well, she wrote back saying, "You are big, tall and fat, but you are very young. . . ."

During the end of that year, Mr. Russell went to inspect schools in my district, and both Maynard and I accompanied him as carriers. Where roads were available, we drove, and where there were no roads, we hiked. This gave us a chance to visit our home and our families.

During my last year at Livingstonia my mother had gone to visit her father at Deep Bay, only about twenty-four miles away from Livingstonia. She had the children with her, Nthembwa, Kapampa, and Masida. About two weeks after she came to see me at Livingstonia, she left Deep Bay for home. Toward the end of, I think, the sixth week I received a letter from Mr. Mbale, the clerk to the District Commissioner at Karonga. It was one of those OHMS (On Her Majesty's Service) envelopes, and my friends were standing around to hear what it was that merited me an official dispatch. It was a report that my mother had arrived at Karonga a few days ago and had gone to the hospital with Masida, sick with malaria, and that only two days later, Masida died.

In our last year of school, after all those cold and wet years, we were ready to go home. We were given another pair of uniforms with the school motto on the left pockets of our shirts saying, I WILL TRY. We loved the motto, and we were proud of it, and we were going to try in our endeavors. Perhaps some of us would meet again, perhaps some of us would go on to colleges, it was just perhaps. We did not know, but we all knew and would repeat the motto, "I will try."

I had made many friends in those few years, and I remembered my mother's words as we were parting, "Be friendly and they will be friendly to you." Those boys had helped me in many respects, but in what way did I help them? I did not know. But they were still my friends, and I was sad to be parting from them. Never again would we all gather together as we were then, never again would we be so happy together. We had lived together as one people belonging to one school, but now if we were to meet again, we would very likely meet as different people belonging to different institutions.

That same last week of school, we all had the opportunity of hearing an address by Mr. Kanyama Chiume, who was then a member of the Legislative Council. His theme: Imperialism must go. In the course of his speech he gave us a brief account of the arrival into the country of a hero of heroes, Dr. Hastings Kamuzu Banda, who had recently returned to his country from abroad where he had lived for the last four decades, and now he was back in his country of birth to work for its freedom from the bondage of foreign domination. He was back in his country, and his country received him. He was back to his people, and they welcomed him with jubilation. The whole country rejoiced, and we all rejoiced that he, the man we had been waiting for so long, was now back. We were told that he, Kamuzu, would address a meeting at Chinunka, only a hundred miles from my home, two weeks from that day. I would be on holiday then, and come what may, I would go and hear him.

The week ended, the school closed. Home we went. I spent one week at home, then I was ready to take another trip. This time to Chinunka to hear the hero. I was just leaving when I saw a car pull in before the court. It was the District Commissioner himself visiting our area. I asked him if he would give me a lift to Chisenga. "Sure," he answered, "I will be leaving in ten minutes." In ten minutes, as he had said, we were off on the road to Chisenga.

"If I may ask, what are you going to do in Chisenga?"

"I am not going to stop in Chisenga but am proceeding to Chinunka."

"How are you going to get there from Chisenga?"

"Walking, I guess."

"Going to visit some friends there?"

"No, sir."

He was a Government official, and as such I took it for granted that he would certainly be aware of a political meeting of such importance being held in his district, and so I was not going to tell him I was going to a political meeting if I could help it.

"Are you a member of the Congress?" he asked, referring to the Nyasaland African Congress.

"Not exactly. I mean, I am a sympathizer."

"Dr. Banda is holding a meeting there the day after, and maybe while you are there you will have time to go and hear him."

"Sure I will hear him. As a matter of fact, that is why I am going there."

"Are you a student?"

"Yes, sir."

And we talked, as he drove on a narrow winding earth road. "So you want to be a politician," he continued. "We are not as bad as your politicians tell you. Look, we gave independence to Ghana, and we shall give you your independence when you are ready, not now."

"You mean we are not yet ready for it?"

"Of course you aren't."

"And when shall we be ready?"

He only shrugged his shoulders.

We talked, and he drove on that same narrow winding earth road. At Chisenga he dropped me off, and I walked to Chinunka.

The day arrived when our hero would address us. It was a cloudy and chilly morning. "It is going to rain," I sighed, but the gods were going to hold the rain up there until we had heard our hero. Hundreds of people gathered on an open field, and many were still gathering, and still many more were coming. Here people danced, there people beat drums, and over there they sang "God Bless Africa." But the doctor was not yet in. Suddenly we all stopped and cheered. The drummers cheered, the dancers cheered, the singers cheered, and everybody else. "He has come," we shouted, "the messiah has come." Dr. Banda stepped out of his car, followed by Mr. Chiume, then Mr. Chisiza, and others. "Freedom," we shouted, as our dignitaries walked to the stand. "Freedom, *Kwaca* (dawn), Freedom," we shouted, and the hills on the east and the hills on the west all echoed back, "Freedom, *Kwaca*, Freedom . . ."

He began speaking as soon as we had quieted down, and I jotted down his words as he spoke, so I could tell others at home what he had said. "We want independence now," he said. He stressed the importance of unity, yes, like the ancient sages who ascertained that in unity there is strength. With that unity we could not fail to attain our goal, we would even move the giant of mountains. He spoke and we cheered. He was our leader. I wrote down, "He is a strong man. He speaks with the eloquence of Winston." (I was referring to Sir Winston Churchill, whom I had heard was a great speaker.) He finished his speech and we cheered even more, sang louder, drummed harder, and danced stronger. He clapped and we cheered, and that was the end of the meeting.

II

The Road to America

CHAPTER 4

I Have a Dream

I WAS sitting on the verandah of a friend's house that afternoon, wondering whether or not I was going to the malipenga dance the following morning. Malipenga is a kind of dance that is performed by the male members of the community between June/July and October. One community competes with another, and the community that dances best (according to some standards of judgment) wins. Then I began wondering about my final examinations. Did I pass them? They were hard, especially that general science paper. Sitting beside me was an old friend, Kaliyokha, the owner of the house and a nephew of my mother. He was now a man, a man with a wife and child. Eight or ten years ago I used to play with him, but now he was a man, and I was still a boy.

"Did you pass your exams?" he inquired, as though he had been reading my thoughts.

"I don't know," I sighed. "The results are not out yet, and it will be two months, I think, before they are out."

"You passed them," he said with assurance, as though to him there was no such thing as failing an examination. "You passed them. I know."

He had never taken any examination himself, having never been to school, and I knew that in a way he did not know what he was talking about, but at the same time I could not fail to be flattered by his remarks.

"Maybe, I have," I said, then added, "I am sure I have passed them."

"You see," he said, "we have confidence in your work."

"That's the whole problem," I said.

"What?"

"People always say they have confidence in you, and if you fail, they laugh at you. They themselves do not like others to have confidence in them."

"What are you going to do now?" He asked that inevitable question, the question we all ask ourselves at one time or another. It is a question that we all have to answer one time or another, one way or another, answer it our own way, and to be effective, on our own terms. "I suppose you are going to become a teacher now, and teach our children," he continued.

Become a teacher! It was not a bad idea. After all, prior to my going to Livingstonia Secondary School, I had thought about becoming a teacher but had failed because of my age. After all, Maynard was going to try and become one.

But I had different plans, plans I was secretly entertaining in my mind, plans that were secret even to my mother but known to a few fellow students at Livingstonia. And what were these secret plans? And why were they secret even to my own mother?

"We shall meet in America," I remembered saying in our dormitory at Livingstonia.

"Shall we?" the boys would answer sarcastically. "When will that be, now?"

"I am just dreaming," I would dismiss the subject.

One of our textbooks in literature was Booker T. Washington's *Up from Slavery*. During my first year at that school I found that one of the senior boys was nicknamed Booker. I learned later it was because of his material poverty. When later I stood to fill his shoes, I could feel no pride. It was not a compliment. It could only be a compliment if I could do like Booker, if I could rise up to his heights.

I remembered Harton Mwakikunga, a fellow student. I could see him again, sitting on the short grass outside our dormitory, with his back toward the sun. He would read, read anything that came his way, and yet find time to read his textbooks and beat us all in the class.

"This is what I call a good example of the law of survival," he would sigh after finishing reading some book.

"What example?" we would ask.

"Robinson Crusoe," he would answer.

"What about him?" we would query him.

"Read boys, read," he would get angry. "Read. Here it is."

Or sometimes, after a long reading, he would begin briefing us on what he had read. "Now," he would begin, and we would listen attentively, expecting to hear some of the odd stories of Perseus or Jason or Crusoe. He told these stories with such a feeling that you would suppose he was speaking from firsthand experience. "Now," one day he began, "this is what I call real faith, the faith that really helps one to strive to his goals."

"And what is it now, Harton?" We would ask him to explain what it was that he called real faith. He read avidly, and whatever he read, he could relate it to something else, or find some connection to something else.

"Well, Abraham Lincoln," he said. "He was born a very poor man, poorer than most of us here," he said, looking around us. "But he had faith in God and in himself, and see what he did."

"What did he do?" we would ask, revealing our ignorance.

"Read boys, read," he would lose his temper. "Don't just sit down here as if you can't read."

I had been very much impressed by his account of Lincoln. I had never dreamed that there was a person who was poorer than I was, yet who in the course of his life had ac-

complished much more and far above the powers of my am-
bition. I had always thought myself poor. I had always pitied
myself for being so poor. Indeed, I had too often used my
poverty to explain my inability to do something. "I am poor,"
I would always excuse myself, "what can I do?" I felt very
ashamed for having allowed my material poverty to impede
my school work and any other work. Perhaps, I thought, it
is not too late to correct the situation.

One morning, one of the boys had come into the dormitory
panting. "Boys, show where Ghana is on the map," he said.
We did not know where it was. That was on March 6, 1957,
and Ghana was born that day. "Gold Coast is independent
today," he informed us. He had gathered the news from a
friend who had a wireless. He told us who the Prime Minister
of the new nation was, where he had gone to school, how
many people live in Ghana, and so forth. We shouted in joy
and assured ourselves we too were on the road to independence.

I saw the land of Lincoln as the place where one literally
went to get the freedom and independence that one thought
and knew was due him. One day I would also go there, I
would also go to school there, and I would also return home
to do my share in the fight against colonialism.

Toward the end of my stay at Livingstonia, we had often
read of students from Uganda and Kenya who went to the
United States for their college work. I had wondered why it
was that few from Nyasaland went overseas for their college work, while these students in Kenya and Uganda, who
already had their own university at Makerere, were going
in large numbers. But no matter how much I wondered, I did
not know where to place the blame. I would go to the
United States, I decided, and perhaps then I would learn the
right place where I would put the blame for the meager
higher education we got. These were my plans. Few knew
them, and my mother was among the many who did not
know them yet.

I had been away from home for some years now, and I feared my mother would not be very willing to let me go away, let alone go to the United States. I knew, however, that she did not know any such thing as the United States, and as a result she would not know where it was or how far it was. Now if I did not tell her until a few days, possibly two days before I was due to leave, perhaps I could persuade her to let me go. If I told her several days before I was to leave, I thought, she would have time to ask other people where this United States was, and she would certainly get some ideas and persuade me to stay home. This, then, was the reason why I kept my plans from her.

"Well, what are you going to do now?" Kaliyokha repeated his question, as we were still sitting on the verandah of his house.

This was my chance, I thought, of learning how I would reveal my plans to mother. If I told him, I would see how he would welcome them and I would thus know how to approach mother.

"I am going to the United States," I said, "to America." I knew he would understand "America" better than "United States."

"Are you mad?" he said, staring in my face as if he were searching my mind to prove his point.

"Why?"

"How are you going to get there? Where are you going to get the money? Who will take care of your mother, the children? Are you not tired of school? What do you want to be, a European?" he inquired. These, I had already thought, were the most likely questions that my mother was going to ask me. If I could convince him, maybe I could convince her too.

"Do you have a pass?"

"What for?" I asked.

"You can't go to Jubeki (Johannesburg) without a pass."

"You can't go to America with one, either. You need a passport."

"Do you have it?"

I did not have it. I would not try to get it. I would go as far as I could possibly go without a passport, and then try to get one. This would probably be a hard way, but I was convinced that for me it was the most direct way. If I had tried for one then, they would have asked me such improper questions as how much money I had, how I was going to travel, or what not, and when I told them I did not have any money, they would say there was no passport for me. I was going to try my luck.

"Does your mother know about this?" he asked.

"I am just joking. I am not going anywhere."

I had returned from the malipenga dance. My mother was home, and everybody else was home. I saw she needed a new cloth, for the one she was wearing was already falling apart. She had been wearing it for some three years at most. Both my brother and sister needed new cloths too, and, moreover, they would be going to school and we needed money for their school fees. Perhaps I was being unwise in deciding to go so far away to America and leave my family in so poor a condition. My mother was certainly expecting me to be a teacher now, and she was no doubt expecting a new turn in her life. To have a son who was a teacher would give her all the pride and the consolation that she had not yet known in bringing him up. She had thanked God she would not worry very much about Nthembwa and Kapampa because I was there to take care of them all. I was going to disappoint her.

Then another man came. He was a teacher at a local school three miles away, the school that I had first attended. I seemed to know the purpose of his visit. He wanted his money.

Three years ago I had no money to return home from Livingstonia during one of the three-week holidays. My former classmates at Wenya, Arlington, Gibson, Neckson,

Kenton, all these were also at Livingstonia undergoing a teachers' training program. They were being paid for their training, and they had contributed some money toward my going home that holiday. So I had come home, but I was unable to return to school. Moreover, I said that I did not like to go back to school because I wanted to pick up a job so I could also buy shoes. My mother had tried to persuade me to go, but I refused. She had gone to this teacher and had borrowed one pound for me. I went back to school, but I had not bought any shoes. Instead I bought her a black cloth, the cloth she was wearing now.

"I have waited three years," the teacher began. "I want my money back."

"I have no money," replied mother.

"When you borrowed the money, you knew you were going to return it. Where did you think you were going to get it?"

I felt very sad. I was responsible for all that. It was for me that she borrowed that money.

My grandfather Tukwewe had cows and I believe he had money too, but Deep Bay, his home, was over a hundred miles away.

"I hear," I called mother, "that the messenger is going to Karonga today to get the mail. I am going with him."

"Where are you going?"

"Just give me some provisions if you have any. I am going to get money from Tukwewe."

"How do you know he will give you money?"

"He is your father, and surely he will sell one of his cows so he can help you."

She had no provisions ready, but I wanted to leave that evening. Kantuwarya, my mother's cousin, lent me three shillings to buy food on the way.

"Look," Kantuwarya said as he was giving me the three shillings, "I am giving you this money, not lending it to you. I want you to tell my uncle that my child died a few days ago before it was born just like the other one. Ask him to send me with you some medicine so my children don't die before they are born."

I ran to the messenger's home but he had already left. I ran after him and managed to catch up with him. We had started the trip very late and it was getting dark already. "We shall sleep at Kopa Kopa," the messenger said.

Early in the morning, long before the cocks crowed, we started out again. We climbed the hills, then descended to the valley, facing the beautiful blue Lake Nyasa. We walked toward it, and slowly it seemed to come toward us, but it was still far away, and the sun was steaming and we were wearing down.

He bought some bananas and we ate them under the shade of a tree, then started out again. Before dark we were at Karonga. The following day I would be proceeding to Deep Bay alone. The messenger wished me godspeed.

I had three shillings in the pocket, and with it I thought I would take a steamer to Deep Bay, only forty-eight miles away, but the steamer had just left for the southern tip of Lake Nyasa and it would be some two weeks before it came back. I went to the market to look for bananas. "Did you go to Livingstonia Secondary School?" someone asked, slapping me on the back.

"Yes, why?"

"I just saw the badge, I WILL TRY."

I kept on walking and the stranger asked me where I was going. Deep Bay, I told him. It was a coincidence, he said, because he was also going there. He had a bicycle and he could take me if I did not have any means of getting there. I should meet him, he said, at the market the next morning.

"My bicycle is about three miles from here with a friend," he said when I met him on the market the following morning. "Three miles," he continued, "is not far. We can walk there and pick it up. Besides, it is on the way to Deep Bay."

I planned to walk to Deep Bay, so walking three miles to

the bicycle was nothing dreadful. But when we got there we found nobody home. My friend said he knew another person who lived another eleven miles hence, and that we could borrow a bicycle from him. When we got there, we found the wife but not the husband and, moreover, they had no bicycle. My friend said that since we had already covered fourteen miles we might as well walk the rest of the way. The woman fixed us something to eat, and we were on our way.

The next day I was at my grandfather's door. I had no time to lose. I told him immediately the reasons for my coming. Two days later he handed me the twenty shillings I wanted and on top of that he handed me a big black cloth for my mother. "I can't give you the medicine my nephew asked for," he told me.

"Don't you have it with you here?" I asked.

"No, it isn't that I don't have it," he said, "you can't carry it."

"Is it very heavy?"

He showed me the medicine. It was no bigger than an ordinary pea, but why could I not carry it? It was dangerous because, he explained, if I had it in my pocket and forgot to take it out when I went to the lavatory, I would never have any children.

"All right, I can't carry it. Bring it with you when you visit us."

I started my journey back home. I had gone about five miles when I met a former classmate at Livingstonia. I asked him if he knew anything about our examination results. He did, and he had failed. It was too bad. In any case, the examinations were hard. I tried to comfort him. Did he know whether I passed or failed? He did not know. I wondered if he knew I had failed but did not want to tell me. Could he tell me the names of those he knew had failed? There were thirty-two in the class and eight had failed. He told me the five he knew. I had little time, so I left him and started on my way. On the way I kept on counting in my mind those that I thought would likely fail, and I would count more than eight of them. "Surely," I would assure myself, "I can't be one of the eight," but then I would add, "I can never tell."

I stopped at Karonga for a day, and during that day I went over to the office of the Inspector of Schools, Mr. Karinga, a former headmaster at Bulambia Senior Primary School.

"I want to see the examination results, sir," I said. "Your name?" the Inspector asked. "Oh, you have passed," he said after I told him. "Here it is." My name was there. I had passed the examinations. How proud Kaliyokha would be! He had said that he knew I passed, and probably he would think he was getting to be a prophet! "You have passed it. I know it," he had said, and now I was saying to myself, "I knew it, I have passed it."

What next? I was going to go ahead with my plans. I was going to tell my mother about my plans, but would she agree, would she beg me to go as she had done three years ago when I refused to return to school? I did not know. I was going to tell her anyway.

"You have passed!" was the cry I received from my friends when I got home. How did you know? Maynard. My mother handed me a letter from Mr. Russell. Accompanying it was a full list of those who had passed. Twenty-four out of a class of thirty-two was much better than the fourteen out of a class of thirty they had the previous year. When I returned from school after my examinations, I had said that the examinations were so hard that if I passed I would be so happy that I would drink my soup right from the floor. They gave me some soup and I poured it on the floor and drank it.

I was now ready to report my plans to mother. I was leaning against a tree, reading a letter from Emma Munthali. My mother was out at the well getting some water. I planned to tell her when she returned, but suddenly there was that sound of the drum, the sound that constantly reminds you that although it is not you today, you too have your own turn, the turn that you can never miss. Even at a distance we could tell that the dead was someone important. It was the mother of our village headman, and the day was October 10. This suggested that I would have to postpone the idea of telling my mother, because she would go to the funeral.

October 12 I was ready to tell her. I just hoped my star would be in the right place. I had two world maps with me, one printed and the other one drawn by myself in my geography class six years before. I was comparing the two maps in the house and I overheard a group of people outside discussing whether I was going to go to Domasi Teachers Training School, and my mother who was among them said she did not know, because I had not talked about it lately. I thought this was my chance, so I went out.

"You are going to Domasi now, aren't you?" one man asked.

"No, I am going to America on Tuesday," I said with all the self-assurance and confidence, and I said it in such a way as to suggest to them my amazement at their not knowing of my impending trip until now.

"Why didn't you tell us?" the same man wanted to know.

"Didn't you know?"

"What do you mean, didn't we know?" my mother wanted to know. "How could we know if you didn't tell us?"

I was glad I had talked to Kaliyokha about it for he was there too, and he broke in saying I had talked to him about it long before I even went to Deep Bay. My mother said that she thought I had told her I was going to be a teacher now. Had she made up her mind? She did not say. There was a heated discussion among them, some saying that if I went to America I would be too educated and I would become too lazy to do anything. "He won't even work in his own garden. He won't even know how to build a house.

You know how lazy these so-called educated people are," they said.

On the other hand, there were those who supported me. Kantuwarya took a stronger stand, saying that if I went to America I would come back an important man. My mother was quiet. I was still lucky because I was the only one who could understand maps at that group. They talked of America as if it were only a few miles away. They wanted to know how I was going to get there. Walk and maybe work on the way, I told them. How long was it going to take me? I did not know. "Five days, maybe?" About five days, I agreed with them, trying to give mother the impression it was not so far away after all.

"Nthembwa and Kapampa will be going to school now," my mother said. "Where do you think they will get their school fees?"

I was going to get jobs on the way and would see to it that sufficient money was sent home each year to finance their schooling. Was it all over? I did not know yet. I had rushingly said that I would leave on Tuesday, October 14, 1958, and there was no changing if I wanted to leave.

That evening I overheard an interesting speech by my mother. She was standing outside our house, all alone, and she was talking. I listened, and she was mentioning my father's name and many other names that I had never heard of before. "Your child is going away," she said. "Give him good luck. Drive away the danger from him. Give him wisdom to return home."

She was going to prepare some provisions for me the following morning, she said. Well, she had agreed. This was a clear indication she had agreed. Funny, I had waited all this time trying to prepare answers to what I thought would be the most likely questions she would ask me even before she considered letting me go or not, but she did not even bother to ask me those questions. To convince her more,

I gave her a speech based on the questions and answers that I had put to myself in her behalf before.

On Monday morning I had my hair cut and I washed my school uniform, the khaki shirt with its I WILL TRY badge and the khaki pair of short trousers. Kantuwarya gave me a white bag in which I would put my flour for food on the way. While at Livingstonia I had obtained an English Bible, and someone in England had sent me a copy of *Pilgrim's Progress*. I was going to take these two books with me. I kept wondering all that day if I had not made one of the wildest gestures. Leave home and decide to walk to America! "That's madness," Kaliyokha once termed it.

Mother began giving me that old advice: "Remember I told you once before. You are going to a very strange place, and you don't know anybody there. I told you before if you are friendly to people, they will also be friendly to you. Help them and they will help you. . . ."

"You know I did that at Livingstonia, mother."

"I just want to remind you," she added. "And God bless you."

"I am counting on that, mother," I said, and a strange feeling ran through my inside. I remembered very well, yes, very clearly, that I was counting on the help of God, the same God I had cursed only a few years before. I was very startled and very frightened that during all those years that had passed since that evening I had forgotten it all and now I should remember. In all those years I had gone to Sunday School, I had gone to church, I had become a Christian and had been baptized, I had worshiped, and had sung the holy hymns, I had mentioned His Name times without number, but I had not remembered that single moment of that evening when my sister lay dead on the lap of my mother's aunt, that moment when I had cursed God for His unkindness, His cruelty for letting my little sister die. "Yes, I am counting on that," I repeated in a strange, queer, and somewhat faint voice, and my mother looked at me in surprise. "What's the matter?" I heard her whisper.

"Nothing, nothing at all." My heart seemed to heave with that strange feeling, *that strange fear*, the fear that I had not only rebelled against God, I had not only rejected Him, but I had cursed Him. "Forgive me," I murmured to myself. I began arguing within whether I had really rebelled against the Lord, and finally I was satisfied with the explanation that if I had rebelled against Him or rejected Him it was only through my ignorance of Him.

CHAPTER 5

I Will Try

I WAS wide awake. The cocks were crowing in almost every house in the village, signaling the break of a new day. "*Kwaca*," I said. Yes, it was the same crowing cock that was the symbol of our national liberation. It crowed and we all knew it was dawn for us all, that we had slept through the long night of colonialism and imperialism, of foreign domination and oppression, and that now it was kwaca, dawn for us all, a new day for us all to begin our new lives, engage in our real activities under the banner and aspirations of freedom as opposed to the mere dreams we had during that long night that we slept in our own house rented to us by the imperialist. Yet also it was dawn to me for different reasons.

I had had a good sleep on a mat of reeds spread on the bare floor. I had had a perfectly all right night, excepting an occasional inconvenience of wondering whether or not I had made an awfully wild and unwise move, whether or not if I really left I would ever return and see the faces of my family and friends. I had all my trip mapped out. I would go as far as Port Said or Port Alexandria and see the possibility of working my way on a ship to New York. But what if there was no such possibility? What if I was not able to go as far as all that? I would always return home.

The sun rose over the mountain as it had done since and

before I was born. The children were running around the
houses already, having their morning play as we all had done
in our days. The little calves were running to their mothers
to have their breakfast, but the boys would not let them
have it until they had finished milking the cows and then the
hungry little calves would be permitted to have the little
milk that was accidently left there after the boys had thoroughly done their morning chore of milking the cows. Men
were sharpening their axes and their spears, ready to go out
into the woods or to the hills to do the men's chores as all
men had done before them for ages yet unknown. Women
were rinsing their pots, preparing to dash to the well to
draw water for use in the houses just like all other women
had done before them, also for ages we never could imagine.
That was the routine, the uneverending routine of happy
children running around the houses, with strings for boys
or strings of beads for girls tied around their waists as if it
were but a uniform for children, with pieces of cloths hanging on the strings in their fronts, now hitting on one thigh
now on the other, as the joyful children ran and laughed;
the routine of men sharpening and comparing the sharpness
of their axes, the routine of women dashing for the wells,
singing as they dashed or gossiping as it is customary among
women; all this was a routine I had not yet broken myself
from. It was also routine, the routine of my forefathers.
Wherever I went, whatever I did, I would always come back
and do this same routine.

But that morning I was not sharpening my axe. My mother
was not rinsing the inside of her pot and dashing to the wells
with her friends. My sister, my brother, were playing as
usual, running and cheering. It was the same day to them.
It was not different from any other morning, and therefore it did not call for any special treatment.

It was that morning of October 14 in the year of 1958. It
was that day I had scheduled myself to pull myself from
this routine of which I was a part, to pull myself out of it,

and yet sincerely hope and pray that someday I would return to it and hope it would welcome me back as a full part. Yes, that is where I belonged, and whatever I would later turn out to be, that is where I would belong even if I would have to crawl coming back into my internized routine, the internized routine of my father and his fathers before him. I could hardly fail to imagine, sadly in a way, that if my plans worked out I would probably return to my place to find these happy children past the stage of milking boys, the milking boys sharpening axes, and, as one can never tell the will of God, some of these men now sharpening the axes, some of these women now rinsing their pots, all gone, having preceded us to the next world as they preceded us, the children, into this one.

The men, with their glittering razor-sharp axes hanging on their shoulders, talked to me for a short time before they disappeared into the heart of the forest and before I disappeared into the heart of the continent, striking for another continent, a continent that to them all was no more than a legend, a legend one hears about from someone who also in turn heard about it from someone else.

"We are allowing you to go," they said to me. But in reality they were not telling me, they were telling their ancestors, my ancestors, that I was leaving the village in good faith and that they, the ancestors who had also sharpened axes and had disappeared into the woods, the ancestors who had also dashed to the wells, gossiping as they did, should protect me on the way and bring me back in good faith such as I had when I had left the village.

My mother had a dish of sima and a dish of cooked chicken ready for me. I took all my time eating it, chuckling to myself as if it might not be the last dish of sima and chicken I would ever have at home. "In all thy ways acknowledge Him, and He shall direct thy paths," I repeated one of my favorite verses.

It was mid-morning when I was ready to leave. I wore

my school uniform and I looked like a schoolboy again. My head all shaved, my feet no more covered than they were the night I entered the world, I stood tall outside our house.

"Wherever you go," my mother said, "I shall always recognize your footprints." She could. Wherever I had gone, and if she passed that way and saw my footprints, she could always know I had passed there, for to her my footprints were as unique and different from any other person's footprints as fingerprints of one person are different from those of another. She handed me my white bag containing flour for the five-day trip to the United States of America, an extra khaki shirt, a blanket, and the two books, the English Holy Bible and the *Pilgrim's Progress*. In my left hand I was holding an axe, my axe. My father had made it for me when I was still a child going to Mpale Village School. I was going to take it along.

I shook hands with my brother and sister and they looked just as happy as if they expected me home in the evening. I shook hands with mother, and she spat on my face, our version of kissing but stronger than that version, for my mother at least. Spitting in my face was not only a token of love and good will, it was also a token of remembrance. I would always remember her. Wherever I went, no matter how many times I washed my face, her saliva would still be in my face, and whenever I looked into the mirror I would see her saliva in my face, and I would know how it came there, and so I would remember my mother. She walked with me for a good part of a mile and she was giving me her old advice. I shook hands with her for the last time, and without a word she started back to the house. I watched her for a moment, then stamped my foot hard on the ground, for every morning she would come and stand there, and she would see my footprint and she would say, "I know who stood here."

Maynard, who was living with his uncles at Sekwa Village, and who knew of my impending trip, came up to see me off. He came in time to see me already on the march, heading for what I always hoped would be north.

"Well, traveler," he joked, "don't get lost now."

"I won't," I said, but I really could not tell. Besides the maps of Africa and the world that I had in the pockets, I would have to depend pretty much on asking people on the way about directions.

"Write me and tell me of your adventures," he said. "Someday I might follow you, who knows?"

"Do you have a pencil?" I asked as I realized I carried neither a pencil nor any stationery. He handed me a pencil, and I could see his white teeth as he smiled doubtfully at my madness.

"If I fail, I can always return home, you know," I said, trying to warn him not to laugh at me in the event that I came home sooner than he thought. After this, and some more silly and unimportant talk, such as that he was now the only fellow with a secondary education in the village, and, my, all those girls would be running after him, we parted our ways, he to the village and to the security of friends and relatives, I to the unknown and the mercy of the wilderness.

As an entry into Tanganyika, I chose the trail on which, years before, I had trod in the company of a few men and cows. I was strong and healthy, and I would trample on the earth with all my strength and my health. I quickened my pace, walking with all the impatience as though I expected to reach America that evening, but that was just the beginning of the longest single journey that I had ever attempted, a journey that originated with the greediness for learning.

I climbed Bula, one of our small mountains, and this was to be the first of the many small mountains and many hills I would have to climb, even before I was to enter Tanganyika. On top of the mountain I sat down to rest, my first rest on the wild journey. I sat on a pile of rocks. Each traveler that had ever rested there would, upon leaving the place, leave a rock of his own, and the pile was now large. I looked down on the valley, my valley, and my home. Many a time I had rested here before, I had looked down on the same valley, but it had never looked so different as it did now.

It was all dry, and the trees had all lost their leaves. It was a matter of weeks now that it was October, when Nature, like a little child that enjoys showing you her new toys, would come, brushing and wearing her new colorful dress. The trees would begin to grow new leaves. Now I could see through the leafless branches of these trees, and I could see well down the little houses spread in the valley. Occasionally I could see a string of smoke rising gently in the broad daylight straight into the heavens, as if to beckon me to return home where I would enjoy the warmth of its fire at night as I had always done when I was a child, sleeping in the barn.

I saw the Didimu River winding itself along the valley, paralleling the mountain range. There, in that river, I knew that once upon a time a mother rejected her child and threw it there to the mercy of the river, but the river had refused to accept the gift. I could see my little school. Strange things happen, I thought, for once I had disliked going to school and had hidden in the forests to play with friends and go home in the evening to tell my folk I had gone to school. Several times I had quit school, and once I had refused to return to my secondary school, yet today I was giving up all to run after that which I had once disliked. Beyond the valley I could see the top of another mountain, Nyikamwaka. I knew that in the bosom of that mountain rested the body of one of my brothers. After this I took a last look at the valley, and after placing my rock on the rock pile, I left.

Chiteka Village was once the home of my mother's father and his relatives. As a medicine man he had been popular among the villagers there. It was there that I spent my first night on the journey, the first of the many nights that

I would spend on the way. I had little trouble getting acquainted with the people.

"*Mzukulu wa Tukwewe,* Tukwewe's grandson?" they would ask with some sort of emphasis as if to suggest that being the grandson of Tukwewe was something special. As a favor to their old doctor, they fed me and gave me room to sleep. My flour thus would last me one day longer. I knew that from this village onward I would strictly be on my own.

By about noon of the third day after leaving home I had finished climbing the last hill in Nyasaland. Once on the top I could see the wide valley below me and also the northern tip of Lake Nyasa. I could see the Songwe River lying like a tiny little branch sticking out of the big tree of Lake Nyasa. Beyond the Songwe River lay Tanganyika, for it was that same river that separated the two sister countries. In a few hours I would climb down to the valley and by sunset I would be in Tanganyika. A group of men joined me there. They were going to Kyela on the other side of the river to buy some things for their families.

We crossed Songwe in a canoe and a few hours later, after crossing Kibira, we came to Kyela. They had reached their destination, but I had merely started mine, and it would be many years before I would also sit down and yawn a proud yawn and say, "I have reached my destination."

It appears they had some connection with one of the Indian traders there because when we arrived, they and the Indian began chatting amicably, and the Indian accommodated us in one of his servant's cottages.

Once more I was alone. I had been on the road for some six days but I was still walking with that youthful vigor. I was beginning to pile up miles, and with each mile Mpale, my dear home, was drifting farther and farther back. Was America drifting nearer? I could not tell. If I were on the right course, it was. I was following a road, the road that would take me to Mbeya, but Mbeya was not my destination. My food was nearly finished, and with this, my luggage became much lighter. But I was to have another problem.

I could not speak Swahili, although I could understand some of it. I would learn. I was not born an Englishman, but I had to learn the English language, and Swahili, which was not so different from my Tumbuka after all, would not be hard to pick up. Cars were whizzing by me. Buses were hurrying their passengers to their destinations, but my destination did not call for any hurrying. The road was becoming crowded with people, walking to both directions. Although I did not know them and they did not know me, at least I was satisfied I was in the company of people. I listened to their conversations, trying to pick up some words, but it was all confusing and varied, for now I would listen to this group here with whatever topic they had under discussion, and now I would listen to that other group with whatever different topic they had under discussion.

There were several little "stations." In these, one would see Indian traders. They had their shops, and people would flock in to buy things or just to look at things, admiring them and wishing one were blessed with all the money in the world so one could buy all those things. I went up to one of the Indians and in my poor Swahili, actually a combination of my Tumbuka and Swahili, I asked him for a temporary job. He had a good many piles of new hoes stacked in sacks and, with a group of other workers, I was to carry them into his store. I accepted the job, the first of the many jobs I was to do on the way. Three days later he paid me three shillings. I wrote home telling them where I was and how I was making out.

Nine days, ten, eleven, and I came to Tukuyu. My mother's cousin was supposed to be working somewhere there, but I did not have his address. He was supposed to be a teacher at one of the smaller schools here, but I did not know the name of his school. Anyway, I still had around two shillings in the pocket and with it I would buy enough bananas to reach Mbeya, where I hoped to pick up another job. I stayed at a market most of that night and then went to some kind of rest house where travelers, mostly bus travelers, stayed. In the morning a man came up to me and asked if he could buy my axe. With the two shillings I had, I did not think I was desperate enough to sell the axe, so I refused.

Sixteen days later I entered Mbeya. I was there already, but I reminded myself that this was only the beginning, for America was still as far away as when my mother was spitting in my face, wishing me good luck. "You are mad, you are really mad," Kaliyokha had said several weeks ago. "Now," I was saying to myself, "I am mad, I am really mad." I Will Try, said my shirt, but it was dirty now, all my clothes were dirty, and I was dirty also. Should I take a bath in the river before I entered the big city? No, the water was cold, and moreover it was a cold day. I would wait, perhaps till tomorrow, hoping it would be fine then.

As I was going to the market to get some bananas, I saw a whole crowd of people. They were dancing and singing, dressed up in the most colorful clothing I had yet seen. I learned that someone was getting married. I joined the crowd of people, dancing with them, but someone complained to me that it was dangerous that I should be dancing in this big crowd with an axe in hand. I left the dance and went back to the market.

I saw, by some strange coincidence, someone whose face looked familiar. I approached him. He was buying rice. He looked like a boy who had left our village some six or seven years ago, but I had been told he was working in Tabora. What could he be doing here in Mbeya? He saw me as I approached.

"Legson?" he shouted.

"Yes, Legson," I said, rather perplexed.

"How are you? What are you doing here?" he asked as

we embraced each other. We sat down and began telling each other of our lives.

"I am going home," he said. "I have been here for some time now, and I am going home soon."

"That is what all you people say," I kidded him. "You say you are going home now, but you never do."

Was I still going to school? No, not now.

"Looking for a job in Tanganyika, eh?"

"Yes, that's right," I said, trying to conceal from him at the moment my plans. "Yes, I am looking for a job."

"You will find it," he said. "You will find it with no trouble at all. Look, I will help you find one tomorrow."

"Calm down now," I said. "I am not looking for a job in Mbeya here. I want to go a little farther into the interior of Tanganyika."

It would be a little hard to get a job in the interior part of the country because of my inability to speak Swahili, he said. It would be to my advantage if I stayed in Mbeya and learned the language before I thought of going any farther in search of a job.

"We shall discuss this later," he said. "Let's talk about home now. How is everybody? Do they remember me? Are all those girls married now?"

"Home," I informed him, "is just as you left it, except that many children have been born, and some of the people you used to know are now dead."

"That's too bad," he said in a low voice, then spoke up rather loudly, "Is the daughter of ———— also married?"

"She is. Did you want her?"

He did not. He was married already to a woman there in Tanganyika. I would see his wife that night, he said, at their little house outside the town.

"Do you remember those good old days?" he asked.

Of course I remembered them, but I did not see much goodness in them. He was born in our village and grew up there. We had played with him, and he was the fellow who had discovered, to our joy, that a burnt piece of bone wrote like a piece of white chalk. But he had also been of quite a different character. He refused to work in the gardens, he refused to go to school after our parents discovered that we were cheating them, and above all he had taken to stealing. He stole chickens and cooked them out in the woods, and then came to the village to steal some more if he was not satisfied. Of him we had sang that "next he is going to steal a cow," but he had not gone that far. Now here he was, asking me if I remembered those old days. Sure I did. I remembered our chickens and the man who stole them. I remembered my father picking up some ashes from the spot where he had roasted his stolen chickens and threatening to take those ashes to a witch, who, he thought, would by his powers use the ashes magically to strike this fellow. Now he was grown up, he was married, and he looked very fine. Maybe he had given up his past ways and was now building himself into a finer man, a respectable man.

"People did not like me at that time because of their chickens," he said with a smile on his face. He might have been reading my thoughts.

"They have forgotten about all that," I said.

"I bet they will remember when they see me."

"They won't do anything," I said, pulling out fifty cents from my pocket. "I want to buy some bananas. I am hungry."

He and a few others had also walked from home to Tunduyu, and there they had caught a bus belonging to a company they were going to work for somewhere in Moshi.

He bought me some bananas and then said, "Let's go to my house so you can meet my wife." We ate the bananas as we were going to his house.

I met his wife, a little pretty woman. She sounded very kind when I met her, especially after her husband had introduced me to her saying, "Besides me, this is the first person you have met right from my home."

"Ah." The wife smiled. "Welcome home."

She left us seated outside the house, talking of life at home, life in Mbeya, and a whole series of topics, while she went inside the house to busy herself with the household chores. Pretty soon she came out to announce that she had the water ready for me to take a bath. I had a good warm bath, the water having been heated by her on an open fire. The bath over with, I came out, to be informed that dinner was ready, a dish of rice and fish. I really was at home.

My friend lent me short trousers while I was having mine washed along with my shirt and the blanket. I wrote my second letter home there, and this time I had much to tell. "I've met ——— and I am staying at his house. He's married now and he's a fine man," I wrote, hoping that in case he decided to go home, they would probably judge him by the account of my letter rather than by the theft of their chickens.

I tried to look for a job. Indeed, with my limited understanding of Swahili, it was going to be hard going.

"Can you cook?" an Indian asked me.

"No job," he assured me when I told him I could not.

Of course, I could cook for myself, but that was different from cooking for somebody else, especially when you cook for him for pay.

One week passed and I still did not have any job. I had, moreover, not yet started learning the language, because my friend and I were always speaking in Tumbuka. However, I could understand it better than before. Almost two weeks passed before I got a job sweeping an Indian's store in the morning. I worked there for two weeks and he paid me five shillings, which I thought was not so bad.

It was already December. If I had just given my mother the address of that place, probably she would have written me by now, but I did not give her the address because I did not think I would stay there that long. I would spend my Christmas with my friend and his wife. Moreover, it was raining hard those days, and it would be a bit difficult now to walk as fast as I had done a few weeks before. I WILL TRY, my shirt said, and I repeated the words to myself as I had done several times. After all, I told the people at home that if I had trouble on the way, I would always return home. No doubt, they would laugh at me if I did return, but at least I would tell them that I tried. I tried to find another job, but failed. I wrote home again, saying I was still in Mbeya, but would be leaving soon.

It was now Christmas. People were rejoicing, but I was thinking of my trip and America. "I will get there," I said. Maybe two years, maybe three or four or five years, but I will get there. My friends prepared meat, rice, fruits, and bananas for our feast on this Holy of the Holy days. We ate and rejoiced that in faraway Bethlehem, Christ was born. The Saviour, the Messiah, we say, was born in Bethlehem. "Still the night . . ." People sing in their own language, but it is the same "Still the Night" that I know. I hummed along with them. I ate bananas and hummed with them. I ate a lot of bananas those days. When I was at home I ate bananas maybe once in a full year, but now I ate them twice or thrice a day.

"Are we going to church?" I asked my friend and his wife.

"No," they said. "We shall stay at home and enjoy ourselves here in the house."

The day was over and Christmas was over too. Well, that is one of its beauties: it comes only once a year.

"Next week I am leaving," I said.

"Where to now?" they asked.

"To Chunya. To look for a job at Chunya."

January came, and with it the New Year. I wrote home that I was leaving Mbeya, that it would be some time before they heard from me again. The year was only two days old and I picked up my things to strike forward into the unknown world. I did one thing rather unwise before I left. I exchanged my axe for a small knife.

I had at most four shillings left in the pocket. With it I would buy a good many bananas. With a knife in the pocket, a bunch of bananas in the bag together with my books and the blanket, and a stick in hand, I left, whistling and swinging the stick around. I unfolded the map and there ahead was Chunya, my next destination.

I stopped for some time at one of the villages that day and ate some of my bananas. Since I was assured that the next village was not far, I thought I would get to that village and spend the night there. I left, but I regretted it because it started raining, and most of my bananas got spoiled because they were already overripe, and I could not have eaten all of them at once as they were many. I remember very clearly when a little animal crossed the road a little way ahead of me. I could not see it very well to determine what it was. I was frightened. I quickened my pace, and when I came to the spot where I thought it had crossed, I did not even care to stoop down and examine its footprints. Maybe it was a deer, I later told myself. A deer! how proud it would be if it knew I was scared of it.

It was during the second day that I finally reached Chunya, having been forced by rain to spend the night at one of the villages not very far from Mbeya.

I had less than three shillings in the pocket when I got to Chunya. I would try to get a job there, and if I did not get it, I was still in good shape. I would buy bananas to last me a good many days. I saw a house that was being built. *"Kazi?"* one of them asked. *"Ndiyo,"* I said. They gave me a job. I would be carrying bricks from where they were heaped to where they were building the house, and working with me were several men. I suppose they were local men there. I did not realize then how many times I would carry bricks before I finished my journey.

One day a man asked me where I was from. No one these

days would understand me if I said I came from Mpale, but they would understand Nyasaland. I learned that the man himself was also from Nyasaland, from Mzuzu. We talked for some time. He was working in Chunya too. Nyasa people are scattered all over Africa, he said, and added, "We Nyasas have a taste for traveling."

"Yes, we do," I agreed with him.

Eighteen days had now passed since I arrived there. It was about time I started thinking of leaving again. I had not written home for a long time, and I did not know what they were thinking. Maybe they thought I was dead or lost. They had heard from me, but I had yet to hear from them. Maybe they were well and sound. It was raining very often those days, and that would not be very good for me. I could wait there for another week or so; there was no need to hurry. America was still very far, far away across Africa, far away across the Atlantic. If only the rest of the way would be as smooth as it had been so far, I would reach America.

It was toward the end of February that I finally left Chunya for Itigi. Friends there were telling me that the best way was to follow the road. I had no compass, and I could easily get lost, they said. However, they also advised me to follow the trails sometimes because "there are villages scattered in these woods you see," and if I followed those trails I should be able to go from one village to another in a relatively short time, so that if it got dark or if it started raining again, or if I was simply tired and needed a rest, I would be able to find a village and there protect God's soul. With this advice we parted, they to stay and carry bricks, and I to resume the journey toward another continent. There was no hurry.

I followed the road for what I thought was three hours, I had no watch to be able to say exactly how long, and now I branched off the road. It was easier to find one's direction on the road, I admitted. There on the trail one could easily

get lost. I would depend very much upon asking the villagers
as I went along.

I sat down under a tree to rest. The ground was still rather
wet from the rains of the previous weeks. I opened my bag
to pull out some bananas. While eating them I began reading
Pilgrim's Progress. "I walk by the rule of my master," says
Christian to Formalist and Hypocrisy. "You walk by the
rude working of your fancies." I had read this book several
times, and I wondered if I were not myself walking by the
rude working of my fancies!

I was nearing a village, as I could tell from the noises I
heard. I would stay there for the night, as it was already getting late. I could hear them singing or dancing, or I do not
know what. As I approached the little village, I could see
children running around the houses, making the noise. They
stopped their game when they saw me and stared. One went
into the house, possibly to report to the men of the village
that a stranger was coming. A man came out of the house
and he and the children stared at me as I timidly approached.
They welcomed me. The sun was low, they told me, and I
could stay there for the night. I asked them how far they
thought it was to the next village. It was not far.

The children resumed their game and I watched them, reminding myself that I was once a child too, and I did the
same things. It was dark, and they took me to a house where
four boys were sleeping. There was a big fire burning. I did
not fear any cold at night because I could tell from the pile
of firewood that there would be fire all night long. I sat in
front of the fire and pulled out my *Pilgrim's Progress* again.
"And if you will go along with me," says Christian to
Obstinate, "and hold it, you shall fare as I myself, for there,
where I go, is enough and to spare." I am going to America,
I said to myself, and there too, where I go, is "enough and
to spare."

I heard the cocks crowing just as they did that October
morning when I left Mpale. I was not going to start off so

early, but would wait until my friends were up so I could thank them for their hospitality. It started out to be a very fine morning, everything was clear, and the sun came out with all its fury. That was quite a change, for it had been raining much lately, and in many cases whenever it had not been raining it had been cloudy. But not that morning. I was sitting outside ready to go. I heard the music of the birds in the woods, and occasionally I saw a few fly over us. I heard a dog barking somewhere in the woods, indicating there were houses there too. Down the little stream I heard that old chattering of a few monkeys. Maybe they had been invaded. I thanked my friends, but they told me to wait so they could cook me some food. I waited and they prepared me sima, to which I helped myself. They took my bag and walked with me a little way off from the village, and they gave me the directions. They gave me back my bag, and with a kind look that suggested "Good luck" they turned and went back to the village and I went forward.

Of course it was a fine and clear morning, but there was a lot of dew. The trail, which was very narrow and undoubtedly not very much used by the inhabitants around there, passed through a whole area of grass, tall grass, and at such an early hour and wherever the height of the grass permitted I would see this whole area of grass heavily laden with this morning water, and the grass would lean down silently as if a net were spread over it.

It was a beautiful sight, but the grass covered my trail and I had to guess in most cases where the trail lay. I had to use my stick, hitting the grass before me, thus getting rid of most of the dew. Not being able to see where I was stepping, once in a while I would hit one of my toes against a rock, and cursing and swearing I would stop to examine the bleeding toe. At one point, I hit my right big toe. This was the same toe I had once hit against a rock when we were returning from Bulambia several years before, and since then the nail on it had really never come back to its normal shape.

Now I had hit it against something again. I could not stand it. With my eyes closed, my teeth firmly clutched together, and holding my foot with both hands, I sat down on the dewy grass and wept like a little child.

I came to another village, but it being a little past noon and there being no reason to detain me there, I proceeded after asking the people the way that would take me back to the road.

I was walking on the road, a dusty road just like the one at home. On both sides of the road were trees. They stood tall and thick as far as they went. I was walking on this dusty road; really, with most of my toes bleeding, I was hobbling. Once in a while I would look back at my footprints, and I would grieve to myself that these footprints would soon be washed away by the waters of rain, or they would soon be swept away by the broom of wind, and more grieving was the thought that my mother would never come here and see these footprints and say, "I know who passed here."

There were three men walking in front of me, going in the same direction. They were all carrying spears. Most likely they were hunters. I was swinging my stick and hobbling courageously, but they did not seem to take any notice of me although they had seen me. They seemed to be slowing down their pace, and to let them know that I was not particularly afraid of them, although I was, I was not going to slow down my pace.

As a result I caught up with them and then I slowed down. One of them asked me something, but I did not understand. He asked again, and I told him where I was going, hoping that that was what he wanted to know. He asked me something else, pointing at his spear, which I understood to mean that he wanted to know why I was not carrying a spear as they did. I replied in my imperfect Swahili that I did not have any, to which they all laughed, indicating perhaps that I had misunderstood them, or perhaps they were laughing at my stupidity of walking alone in the woods without carrying any weapons. I walked with them down the road, answering their questions and they laughing at my mistakes. No doubt they were very much amused at my misuse of their language. They were going home, I learned, and in a short time they would be there.

They were nice people in their village. All the people I met on the way were very kind. They prepared some food and put mine in a different basket. I thanked them, but hungry as I was, I did not care very much that the meat was undercooked and unsalted. There were quite a good many girls around, beautiful too, but no sooner was I thinking of them than I remembered my mother saying to me, "Leave the girls alone."

The moon was shining now. I had not seen it for several nights because it had been cloudy. The stars in the heavens were twinkling as they have always twinkled. We were sitting around a fire outside, and they were talking of what they had been doing today. I told them what we did at home and they laughed, either because what I told them was funny or because of my poor Swahili, I do not know, but they were laughing all the same. One asked me if my father had spears, and I told them he was dead, to which they seemed sad, showing that they understood me. I added, however, that when he was alive he had spears and he liked hunting too. I told them that when I was home I used to go hunting with the men, and I told them the story of the pig we hid in a river after we had killed it only to find that the flooded river had swept it down river, and they laughed louder. Another asked if I had a wife. They laughed still more when I told them that I was still too young to have a wife. One asked if I could give him my shirt, but I was afraid, I was going so far away and I might be in need of a shirt before I was finished with my journey.

I felt sad that I should not be able to sacrifice a shirt to people who were so kind to me. But under the circumstances this was certainly out of the question. Perhaps, if there were some stores nearby, with the three or four shillings I had in the pocket I would have bought him a simple but colorful shirt, which as opposed to the khaki shirt would have been much in line with the many fancy colored clothes that I had seen so far in Tanganyika. I only hoped that he understood my honest reasons for being reluctant to give him the shirt.

We slept in a small room, and there too was fire. I did not need any blanket and, moreover, nobody else in the room had a blanket. There was a small mat spread on the bare floor, but I preferred to sleep on the floor. One asked if I should like leaves to be spread down there, but I was going to be all right I assured him. It was a quiet night, except that once in a while one would hear what I thought were the laughing hyenas. With my toes sore, I thought I would not be able to go anywhere the following day. When they invited me to go out with them the next morning, I declined the invitation because I needed some rest.

Some three days later, after thanking them for their kindness and friendliness, I started out again. I began following a trail and very soon came to a stream. I took a quick dip into the cold water and left, not caring to stay there long. I remembered what my father had once told me. One should not stay too long near rivers when one is out in the forest because that is where one is likely to meet animals. He had said that if one were traveling at night one should pay much attention to the croakings of the frogs because "when you hear frogs croaking, and then suddenly they stop, you know that something has frightened them into silence, and therefore you should yourself be getting prepared for whatever it is that frightened those frogs to silence." One other advice he had given me along this line those many years ago was that a howling jackal meant that the King of the Jungle himself was exploring his kingdom within the neighborhood.

I had not gone very far from that stream when I saw with awe four or five giraffes. This was the first time I had seen one, and if it were not for their long necks, which of course were not as long as I had pictured them, if it were not for those necks I would not have recognized them. Keeping to my path, and not interested in disturbing them, I stopped for a moment to admire them. Now I was aware that I was passing through the Kingdom of the Animal land. A moment later I was even more frightened when I saw the grass shake and wiggle not very far from where I was. Pretending to be courageous I kept on whistling some odd tune while keeping an eye at that spot when I saw with some delight that there was an animal there and that the animal had horns. Clearly it was no lion. I cleared my throat proudly as though I had just won some major victory, and at the same time I did not fail to quicken my pace.

I was no longer walking, I was running. I had to get to the next village in good time. I could not tell how far it was, but having seen those animals, I could only guess that there was no village nearby. I believe my guess was right for I walked and ran for several hours on end before I was able to come to an area that showed any signs of habitation. It was already past sunset when finally, panting and pitifully exhausted, I entered a village. The people there did not seem willing at all to help. They did not show any signs of understanding me, but I could go no farther. I had to stay there that night, or if they did not want me to stay I would have to find a spot somewhere just outside the village, hoping that in the event that I was attacked at night by some animals I would be able to run back into the village in time to save myself. In such a case I would most likely bring the danger with me into the village, and the villagers, while defending themselves, would also defend me. They did not chase me away. I was a stranger to them, and the fact that we could not understand each other made my status of being a stranger to them a total one. I could feel that they were frowning on my strange intrusion into their affairs, their kingdom, but I was too exhausted to go any farther, and nothing short of violence or force was going to push me out of there.

I sat down under a tree with my back leaning against it. There was a fire burning and a group of children and a few men, at least no more than four of them, were sitting around the fire. There was a heavy silence. I could see that they were all looking at me, probably, I thought, examining if I were an enemy coming into their village with intent to attack them or steal their things. They would turn and look at one another as if wondering why I was not armed. For my part I had utterly failed to create some signs that would convey to them that I was a peaceful person, that I did not mean them any harm.

One of the men began talking, and I guessed he was talking to me because he was looking at me. It sounded as if he kept repeating the same sentence over and over. I tried to tell him in Swahili that I did not understand him, but it appeared he did not understand me. I tried English, to no avail, and desperately I even tried to tell him in my own language. Then there was that heavy silence again. Finally they began going away into the houses one by one. The man that had been talking to me stood up and walked two or three steps toward me. He said a few words and turned back. Slowly he went back, talking as he did, then stopped again and looked at me. I was most pleased to hear "*Jangu,*" meaning "Come." He said this with force, as though he was angry at my not understanding him.

"*Jangu,*" he repeated, but I hesitated to rise and follow him, fearing that I had misunderstood him. Then timidly and hesitantly I rose, picked up my bag, and followed him. I slept in the same hut with him. I suppose normally he slept there alone. He lay down and hummed, and occasionally spoke looking at me, then resumed his humming when he failed to get a response other than an understanding smile. I huddled myself up against the wall a good three or four feet from him. Now I was getting afraid of him, but my fears ended with a long and quiet sleep disturbed only by the noise of, I thought, the laughing hyenas.

I had not had anything to eat when I arrived. I had run out of bananas sometime before, and since I was following an old trail I had had no chance to buy any. I still had two shillings in the pocket. I left the village before noon of the following day. I could not ask any directions because we could not understand one another. I knew I had the road on my left, to the west of me. When I left the village I took the trail that pretty much led in the general direction I would have taken if nothing else forced me to change trails and go toward the road. My aim was to head as much north as my map directed me. However, today my map was not of much help. Itigi was listed on it, but there were no trails leading to it. I would have preferred to walk on the road, where I probably would have been able to buy something to eat, but I did not know how far the road was from my trail. There was no trail that would take me to the road, and I did not want to found my own.

I suppose I could have made my own trail, but having had nothing to eat, and not being sure of the distance, I feared I would become too weak to walk and be lost in the woods. If I became weak I preferred that it occur on a trail so I could struggle myself back to the last village I passed. With this in mind I followed the trail, which was in no way leading to the road. I was startled then when I found myself on the road. The road itself had curved toward my trail!

I had walked for several miles and two or three hours, but I had not yet found any place where I could buy food. I had not yet come to my village. I was getting weak and I sat down under a group of trees and slept for what was probably a whole hour. Of course I was still hungry when I got up from my sleep, and I was thirsty. I was thankful, however, that I was now treading flat ground, which I thought much easier than ascending and descending hills as I had been doing not many days before. I resumed my walking, and when I realized that the road was not taking me any nearer to an inhabited place, I began looking for a trail that would take

me out of the road. I was not able to find one. As I was
walking I heard a burst of laughter not many yards behind
me. For a moment I did not see any people when I looked
back, then I saw a few children running away into the woods.
I was not going to follow them right away for fear their
seniors would attack me, thinking I was chasing their children with intent to harm them. However, either I waited too
long, or the children ran away too fast, for I was not able to
catch up with them. When I came to the spot where I
thought I last saw them, I saw no trail. I walked for a few
minutes toward the middle of the woods, often stopping to
listen. I did not hear them. Suddenly I came to a small trail
that ran somewhat parallel to the road. Even there I could
not tell which direction they had gone. I decided to go north
with the trail.

It was not more than thirty minutes after I began following the trail that I came to a cleared place. There were five
little houses standing in that cleared area, and a few people,
mostly women. It was still daylight and I would have proceeded if it were not for the fact that I was hungry and
thirsty and weak. I noticed as I approached the village that
there were two men, young men, who were dressed in shorts
and shirts and shoes. One of them greeted me in Swahili.
Now that I knew I could communicate in Swahili, although
my knowledge of the language was still imperfect, I lost no
time in explaining my situation. I assured them I would be
willing to pay for my food. One of the two gentlemen said
he would ask the women if they would give me something
to eat, and that if they would not, then he would ask them
if they would sell me some food. This he did, but for some
time the women seemed very hesitant, and while they were
tossing over and over again in their heads the question sub-
mitted to them, I asked the gentleman if he would get me
some water to drink, which he kindly did. While the women
were still talking among themselves, discussing what they
were going to do, I had the opportunity to talk to the two

men and I asked if there were any villages nearby. Their answer was confirmed by the noise I could hear not very far off. One of the women prepared me some sima, and one of the two gentlemen, who were acting as interpreters, informed me that I would not have to pay anything.

There was a village not very far ahead of me, I was assured. There I would find a kind people and there would be a few people who probably would be able to understand me because the village itself was a little larger than where I was now. That was all right, but I wondered if the gentlemen would walk with me to that village. Though unwilling at first, they agreed.

The people in the new village were indeed understandable, and after I had been introduced to a few people by the two gentlemen who had walked with me, I really felt at home. They respected strangers and, as I learned later, they believed that "if a stranger comes to your place, treat him as best as you can. You never know, maybe you will also be a stranger at his door tomorrow."

I had developed some blisters on my feet for the first time since I left home and I would have to remain in the village for several days, if the villagers would allow me to do so. After I had shown them my blisters and explained my desire to rest, they seemed anxious that I should do so. Itigi was not many days away now, but since I had found a people that were willing to help me I was going to remain in the village until I was able to go forward.

I still thought about my family and all the people in my village, wondering how they were and what they thought had become of me. Of course they would not think I was already in America, except mother who probably only wondered why I was not there already. I had not written them for many weeks, and I feared that maybe they thought I was lost. I would have written, but there was no post office.

I stayed in the village nine days. The two gentlemen from the other village sometimes visited me, and sometimes I went

with them back to their village for a short visit. The people
in my new village were building a house. Although I was not
much of a builder, quite often I would be there building it
with them. They were kind people, and they fed me as much
as they fed themselves, and I was sad to part with them when
the time came, but if I was able to leave my family back at
Mpale, so I was going to leave them here.

While there I had had much time to read my books, and
once in a while some of them, amazed at my ability to read
them, would ask if I could teach them this amazing art so
they also could be able to talk with books. It is hard enough
already as it is to teach one a foreign language and to teach
one to read a foreign language when one does not read already. Especially when the teacher and the student do not
have any common language it is doubly hard and doubly
complicated.

They showed me what they considered to be a short cut
to Itigi, for they themselves had often gone to Itigi. They
even tried to talk me into buying a spear, but I did not think
I needed to arm myself. This reminded me of those old days
at home when we used to carry spears whenever we were
going to Karonga, traveling through Kopa Kopa and the
Kamuguze hills where lions and many other wild animals
were supposed to be very common. Normally a person carried more than one spear, and there were times, though not
often, when one would go on that trip without arming himself with any spears, and whenever such a person met some
other person who happened to carry spears with him, the
person with spears would give the person without any spears
a good beating because he thought he was traveling danger-
ously, and after this beating he would give him one of his
spears and wish him godspeed. I admired their suggestion that
I should buy a spear from them so I could protect myself on
the way, but I had feared that carrying a weapon on me
would give terror to people that I met on the way, and maybe

that terror that would befall them as a result of my being armed would prompt them to attack me first.

It was in March when at last I arrived in Itigi. There were some Indians living there, and wherever there were Indians one could be sure there were some stores. There was a railway line, although I could not tell where it came from or where it was going. I bought some stationery and wrote home saying I was fine. Then I picked up a newspaper only a few days old which headlined the political disturbance in Nyasaland. Dr. Banda, the paper said, had been arrested along with hundreds of other congressmen, and they had been detained. The paper went on to say that they had more troubles in the northern province, which is my home province. I wondered if my mother was safe. She was no politician and she had nothing to do with politics. There were many soldiers in the country, the paper said.

Angry and disappointed I sat on the cement floor of the verandah of one of the Indians' stores and talked to myself. These British came to our country and said they wanted to civilize us. Now they arrest us, imprison us, and even kill us. We want to be free, we want to be free like many other countries. We want to manage our own affairs. Why do they not mind their own business in their own land? We did not invite them in the first place; we did not send a delegation to their land and say we wanted them to come and boss us, govern us. They came on their own, and we are not wrong in inviting them to leave the affairs of our land to us, certainly we are not wrong.

I was worried about my family, knowing that they had more troubles in the north. I wanted to stay in Itigi until my friends at home wrote and told me how my family was. But the paper said that most of the roads were damaged and this meant that even if my friends were to write, assuming that my letter was able to get through to them, it would take a long time before I received an answer.

I bought a few bananas and a razor blade. After eating my

bananas I sat on sand and gave myself a haircut. People were watching me and probably wondered what sort of person I was that took the trouble of giving himself a haircut. I did not have any mirror with which to judge my expertness. I was not, however, cutting my hair so I could look smart and handsome. Rather, I was cutting it to get rid of it, in order that my head would be light and I would not have to wash it. This done, and after running my hands rapidly back and forth on my head, I proceeded to another store to see what things they had there. I saw a picture on a calendar hanging on the wall. It was a picture of a man, a little man wearing a loincloth. It was a picture of that great spiritual and political leader, Mahatma Gandhi. I gazed at it for some time, and I thought it funny that I should see that picture only a short time after my soul had struggled violently in anger and rage against Europeans in Nyasaland.

"Do you know him?" interrupted the owner of the store, an Indian, who had been watching me.

"Yes," I nodded my head. "Yes, I know him."

"Good man," he said.

"Yes," I agreed.

"He's a great man," he said.

"Yes, he was a great man," I said.

"A great man," he said again. "He liberated us, you know." He began recalling the history of the making of his country, and not being much of a historian myself, let alone the history of India, with which, for all practical purposes, I was infinitely unfamiliar. I began to feel rather uncomfortable, for I saw that the conversation was dying, since I was not able to do anything beyond putting on a wide smile purporting to convey my agreement or, better yet, my fascination with his thorough acquaintance with his country's history. I have known few men who have appeared unpleased with such smiles, and in virtually all cases such men have understood such smiles.

"Where are you from?" he wanted to know.

"Nyasaland."

"Running away from troubles, I suppose," he said, putting on a faint smile. "Here it is," he continued, unfolding a Swahili newspaper.

The paper was saying the same stuff that I already knew. Then he wanted to know if I knew Dr. Banda.

"Once I attended one of his meetings," I said.

"A good man?" he asked.

"Of course," I affirmed, and added, "and he's a strong leader."

"They have imprisoned him," he said in his soft voice, again telling me what I already knew.

Considering the situation, with my mind wandering about in my village, searching in this house, now in that, wondering if my family was safe from the foraging soldiers, this was not an excellent subject with which one could engage oneself in an extended conversation, but having already heard him literally recite the history of his land, I was not in a mood to be outdone.

"But is he proven guilty?" I asked.

"Guilty," he said. "I don't think they care whether he's guilty or not. They say he is a trouble maker."

"Yes, they don't care whether he is guilty or not."

The conversation came to a stalemate again. An elder woman, possibly the mother of the fellow, came trotting into the store. Presently they began speaking to each other. To me, it all sounded like a bubble of noises, like a record playing at a speed that is faster than normal. The woman spoke with such a squeak that for a moment I was convinced the two were arguing, but then I saw them laugh rather happily. Well, while they were talking, I would also be thinking of some topic with which to start the conversation once he and the woman were done.

"How about a job, sir?" I began my topic. "A temporary job for a stranded person?"

He did not think he had any, he said rather apologetically.

Moreover, even if he had any job he did not know where I would be staying as he himself did not have any extra accommodation. The latter case, I assured him, was not much of a problem. Itigi was a railway station, and there was a cottage where passengers could stay while waiting for their trains. I would stay there at night provided he would keep my books in his store.

He and the woman began yapping again in their language. What they were saying was none of my business, but although I could not understand them I had a feeling they were discussing my request for a job. There was no job, he said again, but he would let me sweep his store each morning for six pennies.

In a place as small as Itigi, it is as anybody would surmise extremely difficult to get a job even of the kind I was being offered. In a larger place, before accepting a job whose pay one was not pleased with, one would always try at another place, but not here. One shilling would have been much better, indeed for that matter, one would wish it were more than one shilling. He knew I was stranded, broke, as Americans say, and I think that he was giving me that job on a humanitarian basis and not because he really needed someone to sweep his store each morning.

I figured my expected expenses. I would not pay anything for my sleeping in that cottage, but I would have to buy my own food, and of course there was an open space outside the store where they sold bananas and the like. I was going to take the job.

For a while everything went as I had planned. However, one day one of the men working at the railway station discovered that I was not staying there as an expectant traveler, awaiting a train to some destination. The place, he told me, was for passengers, not for stranded persons. I had to beg him to be kind to a fellow African.

"We are brothers," I said. "Let's be kind to one another, and not treat one another like these people treat us."

I began regurgitating politics, but he seemed indifferent. "I have to think of my job," he said.

That's the trouble. We all have to think of our jobs sometimes, making other things of secondary importance. I had to appeal to our supreme common identity because I had my job in mind. Without a sleeping place I would no longer have it. He had to depart from that same supreme common identity because he had his job in mind.

He had a soft heart. I would stay there after all, but it would be my own responsibility if his superiors discovered me there. He became very friendly afterward, and twice I even had dinner at his house. Several evenings I would go there to listen to his wireless. Since it took me a little over an hour at most to sweep the store, I would have a whole day wandering about the yard, or sitting in one of the few stores admiring the merchandise that fate herself had prohibited me from buying. Once or twice a week I would stand on the narrow verandah of the railway depot and watch the hissing train sitting on the rails like a centipede of a most exaggerated size. Then the train would whistle and whiz away. Soon it would all disappear, and as if it were only a mysterious and real injustice of distribution in human woe, I would stand there and wonder why it was me in particular that should be stranded on that verandah, dreaming of a faraway land but not in the least able to get a ride even in such a huge thing as a train. It is demonstrably clear-cut sometimes, more especially on a train, that if one does not have what is required in order to have a ride, one does not have it.

Once the train brought some goods for my boss, and for a good part of the day I and a few other men carried them from the depot to the store, which was not very far away. For this he paid me an extra shilling. I could only wish the trains would bring his goods more often. This way I would earn sufficient money to ride in a train. But this was only wishful thinking, and they are rare moments when it ever becomes true.

By the time I was leaving I had in my pocket two shillings and fourpence. I asked if he could sell me a used sefuliya (a tin pan), but he was kind enough to give me one. It looked somewhat like a hat and it was big enough to cover my head. I would use it to boil or cook whatever raw foodstuff I would gather on the way, and also, as I soon discovered after I left, it would be used as a hat when it rained and, indeed, carrying it on my head was an easier and much less tiring way. I did not neglect to get two boxes of matches. I remembered the days when I was younger and still at home. We would make fire by rubbing two sticks together, but I always had blisters in my hands after that. Also, as it was getting to be a matter of routine now, I bought some bananas to take along.

During my stay there I had inquired very closely from some of the people that I was getting to know well, more especially the man at the train depot, about my possible route north. I was not, in many cases, able to get much help except some general comments. Although some of them had been to some of the places that I would be passing through, they had gone there either in cars or in trains and they did not know much about the villages on the way. Some of the villages were away from either a road or a railway line, and it was through many of these that I was hoping to travel. The man at the depot suggested that it would be advisable sometimes to follow a railroad because several depots were scattered along the line and I would be able to get accommodations. My Indian boss knew even less.

"Good luck," is all he could say as an advice.

Trust in the Lord with all thine heart, and lean not unto thine own understanding. Then shalt thou walk in thy way safely, and thy foot shall not stumble.

Then I turned to my *Pilgrim's Progress*.

OBSTINATE: What are the things you seek, since you leave all the world to find them?

CHRISTIAN: I seek an Inheritance incorruptible, undefiled, and
that fadeth not away, and it is laid up in Heaven, and
fast there, to be bestowed, at the time appointed, on them
that diligently seek it. Read it so, if you will, in my Book.
OBSTINATE: Tush . . . away with your Book; will you go
back with us or no?
CHRISTIAN: No not I . . . because I have laid my hand to the
Plough.

I had already started my journey and had already gone so
far, and there was no reason to turn back. I would go forward. There where I was going I would get an education,
incorruptible and undefiled, and one that would not fade
away. I was leaving my family, I was leaving all my friends,
and I was leaving all that I had at home in order to find that
education.

A knife in one of my pockets, a map of Africa in the
other pocket, a cloth bag with bananas and the two books in
one hand, and a sefuliya in the other hand, I was ready to
leave again for that distant destination. I would still follow
the trails as I had done before, and where necessary I would
take the road or the railroad. With my sefuliya now, I
would, if I were to run out of bananas or such food as
needed no cooking, get such leaves as I thought edible and
cook them and at the same time test Harton's version of the
law of survival.

"Beware of pickpocketers," my Indian boss advised me as
I tucked the two shillings and fourpence into my pocket.

"Don't worry," I said. I found no reason to be aware of
them since I knew that I was not going to travel through
crowded places where pickpocketers would be prevalent.

"Here," he said, "you will probably find this useful." It
was sabuni (Swahili for soap). With a shy smile on my face,
I received the gift. Shy because I felt somewhat ashamed that
I only thought and worried of what to eat on the way but
not of how to preserve my own body. To me, this was the

least of my worries, but as I saw in his expression it was also one of my basic necessities.

> Let the Most Blessed be my guide,
> If't be his blessed will,
> Unto his Gate, into his Fold,
> Up to his Holy Hill.
>   And let him never suffer me
> To swerve or turn aside
> From his free grace and holy ways,
> Whate'er shall me betide.
>   And let him gather them of mine,
> That I have left behind;
> Lord make them pray they may be thine,
> With all their heart and mind.

I said my goodbyes and struck again for the faraway continent, the continent that seemed to beckon me from a distance of a million miles.

It had been several months since I left home, and if my letters did not reach home due to the recent disturbance in the country, my family had by now probably given me up for a dead man or, worse still, a lost man, struggling in the unknown lands, pleading for help with no one to hear me. I was not dead yet, and I was not lost yet. In my sleep my mother still came to spit in my face, and I still stumped my bare foot on the ground. Oh yes, she would come again to see the print left on the ground.

The rains would soon be stopping and they would not be a problem, at least for the next few months. But as before, I would have to depend very much on the people in each mtaa (village) that I entered.

One of the easiest routes would be to follow the railroad from Itigi to Tabora and then to Mwanza, on the southern shore of Lake Victoria. But the shortest route was a straight line to Mwanza which would not pass through Tabora, which was to the west of this line. Yet I was not interested in getting lost in that uncharted route straight to Mwanza.

I would compromise, going to the left a little bit, then to the right, and in the course of zigzagging, go straight.

I headed toward Tura in the Western Province of Tanganyika, hoping that I would proceed to Ndala from there, leaving Tabora on my left side, and from thence go straight to Mwanza. As had been the case during the first few days after my departure from home the previous October, I found that I walked with more ease during the first two days. However, it was not until two days later that I arrived at Tura, spending the previous two nights at two villages where, as a good omen, I had been decently welcomed and accommodated. Having eaten up all my bananas, I bought some more there, and this time a handful of fried groundnuts (peanuts) as well, and since I had arrived there not far behind noon, I continued to Malongwe.

At Malongwe I took my first bath since leaving Itigi, and it was in a cold stream. I began to appreciate the gift of the sabuni from my Indian friend. I made a fire near the stream and for the rest of the night huddled near the fire, my bag as a pillow, trusting myself to the care of the supernatural powers. It was the next day, I remember, when, as I was sitting under a shady tree eating the last pieces of my fried groundnuts, I was stung by what I believe was a wasp. It stung me on my lower left cheek near the ear and buzzed away without my being able to identify it. While at home as a young boy playing hide-and-seek with the other boys, I had many times been stung by wasps and bees, more often by the latter but with more dread for the former, yet as far as I can remember, my body never would swell following a sting by either of these. Now it did. My whole cheek began swelling up immediately after the sting, and in a short time I must have appeared to the townsfolk as if I had mumps. I could think of doing nothing else other than what I had seen my mother do whenever some part of my body would swell as a result of an injury. If I had a sore on my foot or toes, for example, my joint would swell, a mwambavu. I boiled some water, and I would dip some leaves into the hot water and press them on my swollen cheek. I do not know if I can attribute the withering away of the pain and the ultimate disappearance to this unusual way of massaging, but at least it gave me the satisfaction of saying I was able to do something about it myself, although it was several days later that my cheek had come back to its normal shape.

So to be a little extravagant, I suppose, I went to a café one morning two days after I had been stung by that villain of a wasp. Already I had wasted two days just idling about in the town awaiting the ebbing of my swollen cheek. I had spent both nights sleeping on the cold bench in what was a market during the daytime. In the café I was tempted to buy a bowl of rice mixed with a deliciously smelling and, to say the least, most appetizingly cooked chicken. It was the whole shilling that was at stake and willingly I allowed it to change hands. Of course, if I were more rational, purporting to engage in activities where I could obtain the maximum profit, I could have bought bananas, and with a shilling, a bunch of them. But I chose to buy a bowl of rice.

While eating my meal I could not help but remember my first rice dinner. This happened long before I even started going to my small school at Mpale. An older cousin, Medson Kayira (a rhyme in first names), whose father was a teacher and later became our chief, had taken me to his home one afternoon where his mother gave us some rice and some cooked chicken. I suppose they had brought the rice from Karonga lakeshore where his father was teaching and from where they had just returned on furlough. I say I suppose they brought it from the lakeshore because usually we do not grow rice at home.

He had told me a great deal about rice, and although I had not yet seen it, I developed a tremendous appetite for it. One can only imagine how pleased I must have been that finally I was going to have a taste of it.

"There are two rules that one observes when eating rice,"

Medson said as soon as we had squatted down to begin our meal.

"Oh, yeah?" I inquired.

"Yap."

"What are they?" I asked. Then, I seemed to put a great emphasis on rules that had some aspects of ritualism connected with them. Often, what I did not understand I never questioned.

"First," he said as a matter of fact, "the guest may eat rice, but never chicken. The host eats both."

"The second?"

"Only the host breathes when eating rice, the guest doesn't."

That was final. The rules of the dinner I had been hungry for had been told to me. I was barred from the dinner after making a futile attempt to hold back my breath so I could eat the rice. I coughed violently, rather to the immense delight of my cunning host.

Now I ate my rice and my chicken without observing the rules as originated by Medson.

Full to the stomach, and trusting my things to the waiter in the café, I took a wandering walk around the area, admiring the baskets of bananas and other foodstuffs found in their market. I also stopped to admire the Tanganyika multicolorful cloths that women and men wore, most of them with some writing printed on them such as *uhuru*. Of course, it was not a rare sight to see these multicolorful cloths. I had seen them throughout my travel in Tanganyika, and I think if I intended to make myself less alienated, in appearance, I would have procured for myself one of those togas.

After a short spell of rain, the red ball in the heavens lightly covered by the thin evening clouds was sending its last rays for the day. I could see the long shadows of the multicolorful dressed women now homeward bound, balancing on their heads baskets containing the unsold of their merchandise. Slowly the long slender shadows disappeared as the sun disappeared. Perhaps they would return on the morrow. Perhaps this was also their routine just as the sharpening of spears by men and the dashing to the well by the gossiping women was a routine at home. Whatever the case, perhaps they would return too late for me to see their long shadows again.

I returned to the café, hungry now but conscious of the rules of economics that most of us learn by intuition, coupled in most cases with impecuniosity. I could afford a cup of tea and maybe a scone, but (if I may suffer the slings and arrows of rationalization) in a world where to plan for the future is to be rational, one has to act accordingly in order to be in line even if one's future is only tomorrow.

The waiter had once lived at Kilosa he told me. He had met many Nyasas working in the sisal fields there, and he could even recall some names. He touched on the name of one Fadwell Msukwa, someone I knew well and whose home was only a little over ten miles from mine, and who with the rest of his family had later moved into our home. I had gone to school with him once for less than a year, and more memorably still I had danced malipenga against him once and with him later. The waiter remembered him well because they had fought. I felt ashamed and embarrassed to have revealed my acquaintance with one who was remembered only as a fighter, but he said that they had remained friends.

The waiter was living a little way out of town, and if he could make some arrangements, I do not recall with whom, he would allow me to spend the night at his home. I did not hear from him. Two nights spent on what was a market during the daytime was sufficient time to establish in me the sense of security. I spent that night in the same manner.

Several days after leaving Malongwe and heading hopefully for Ndala, I stopped at the fairly large village of Nyamwezi, where I spent the night at the market place. I came to the village in the afternoon shivering with cold and a nasty headache. I had been struck by fever. As soon as I entered the village I asked to be shown to the headman, who, upon seeing my pale face, ordered that I should be taken to a small house, which as I learned soon afterward was a boys' house, and that fire should be built for me. In spite of the glowing fire I continued shivering, refusing even to eat the sima they had kindly cooked for me. Added to the strain of cold I spent the following day groaning with what I think was dysentery and running to the latrine with an extraordinary frequency. For a while I even lay near the latrine itself so as to shorten the running time.

As I have already mentioned, my grandfather was a respected medicine man, and often I would accompany him into the forest where he got the medicine for his clients, carrying on my shoulder a small hoe with which he used to dig up the roots he wanted. He never showed me what roots were medicine for what disease because he always said that he would lower the effectiveness of his medicine if he taught it to others. He said that he had learned his medicine chiefly by accompanying another medicine man and memorizing the kinds of roots or leaves he took and the kind of illness he was trying to cure. I had not learned much from my following him, and all I could think now was that if he were there with me, he would have diagnosed my illness as zegema, explaining it as a change in the water and climate, and I remembered that one of his favorite roots (I hope I am not making them less effective as a medicine by revealing them here) were those of a tree called msoro, but I had no reason to connect these roots with my illness. Anyway, in despair I walked about around the village looking for that particular kind of tree and never found it. I came back to the house and lay down.

"Drink this." I was startled by the voice of the headman, stooping beside me with a bowl in his hand. It had some leaves that looked like spinach soaked in water. I drank it and it had a familiar taste, reminding me of something I had drunk sometime and somewhere in my own home. I could only shake my head and say that our "doctors," although they were trained by different schools and possibly different methods, were similar in their diagnosis of an illness and the medication applied to combat such an illness. It was mbozgo, a medicine of leaves as opposed to roots, but what those leaves were I could not remember, and I would not ask because I had to honor the profession. He would probably tell me, but he would be destroying the effectiveness of those leaves as a medicine for zegema.

"Thank you," I said after drinking it all. Neither the fever nor the dysentery disappeared instantly, but I felt very relieved, precisely because of the thought that although I was now many miles away from home itself, I was not yet lost.

They brought me a slice of pawpaw (papaya) and when I was able to eat it, they brought me some sima again which I ate also.

There were, if I remember correctly, four young men, bachelors to be specific, who were already sleeping in the house where I was put. They were sleeping in one room on four separate little mats. At home during the earlier days several of us boys would squeeze together on one mat. I was given my own small mat and, because of my cold, the spot next to the fire.

Like the other folks in the village, these men were most kind and helpful. When I was sufficiently strong enough to walk with my normal vigor I would go around in their kilabas, gardens which they had cultivated. My family had a garden like other families, and although there were times when circumstances impelled me to cultivate it with little or no assistance from my parents, still it was not my own garden.

Three of the boys had been attending some boarding school, and I had the chance of discussing with them in English some topics of interest. I would ask about the surrounding area and the neighboring villages, and they would talk politics, wagering they would become independent that year. I could hardly hazard such a bet myself, fully aware of the leader remaining locked up in the Queen's Hotel.

I felt very depressed at this period, and often I began to entertain hopes of returning home. I was realizing the futility of the whole thing, that there must be a better way and a better time of doing it. I had not covered even half the whole journey, indeed very far from it, and needless to say I would encounter more difficulties on the way than I had so far, but to return home and give up was not easy. I would have failed. I would have wasted all my efforts to no avail. Better go farther, at least up to Uganda, although it would still be counted a failure of the same degree whether I stopped here or in Uganda.

I would argue with myself that it was better that I should return home and live and laugh and talk about my failure and perhaps make a better plan and a better arrangement, than to keep on pushing and possibly die of illness on the road. I even argued that others would learn about the futility of undertaking such an adventure without any more provisions than I had.

After all, if I returned to my village, who would really care whether I had academic regalia and a piece of paper saying I had a degree from an American college, or even a humble diploma from Livingstonia Secondary School? It would not make any real difference. My father had lived all his life without being able to write his own name. My mother, to use her word, was "blind" when it came to print. What difference then would a diploma or a degree make? After all, they were the same people I would be living with in the village who maintained that an educated person was lazy, that he could not build a house or do any manual work with his hands.

But regardless of whether or not it made any difference with a degree or a diploma or neither, I could not readily stand the ridicule arising from my cowardice. I would have not only failed my goal, but also embarrassed the motto of my beloved school: *I Will Try*. Equipped with nothing better than sheer faith, faith in one's self and one's Creator, Dr. David Livingstone had tried and had succeeded. Equipped with no greater tool than this same faith, Dr. Robert Laws, the author of our motto, had tried amid unknown hazards and had succeeded in establishing the great Nyasaland school, appropriately naming it in honor of Dr. Livingstone. I could not stand equal to either of them, let alone compare my petty ability to their monumental ones, but with their example, I could try. We are told that we should seek in order that we may find.

> The difficulty will not me offend;
> For I perceive the way to life lies here;
> Come, pluck up, Heart, let's neither faint nor fear;
> Better, though difficult, the right way to go,
> Than wrong, though easy, where the end is woe.

But although

> Difficulty is behind, Fear is before,
> Though he's got on the Hill, the Lions roar;
> A Christian man is never long at ease,
> When one fright's gone, another doth him seize.

Thus, my faith in myself and in my goal all renewed and strengthened, I was ready to resume my journey.

CHAPTER 6

"I Have Laid My Hand to the Plough"

I HAD stayed in this village long enough to establish a good acquaintance with the inhabitants. Of course, I had much to thank them for their hospitality. Before leaving I ventured to ask the headman if he would give me some medicine to "inoculate" me against this zegema because I feared that since I had had it once already, chances were that I would catch it again so long as I was in the same area.

"Don't worry," he advised me. "The medicine you drank is sufficient." These people trust their medicines. I do not doubt but that my own grandfather would have told me the same thing. I was holding my shirt in the hand while talking to him, and he saw the line of tiny scars across my chest. As if with a sense of pride in his profession, he smiled. He understood perfectly well their being there, knowing as well as I that they were not there as a mark of beautification of one's chest.

One thing I was particularly interested in avoiding on the way was food, especially fruit, that I did not know or was not sure was edible. I sometimes learned later that some fruits I abstained from were edible after all. However, I once picked up some mushrooms on the way after leaving the village. There were several of them, but I carefully chose three of them because of their superior size. I had hoped I would carry them along, and whenever I came to a place where I could get water, I would cook them in my sefuliya, which I was still carrying. I had seen their kind at home and I had eaten some of them so that I was fairly sure of their edibility and nonpoisonousness. However, I never ate them and I do not really recall what I did with them.

There was one other thing during this period that frightened me almost to the point of losing my wits. It was not an animal or a snake or a man or anything like that. I sat down to rest one clear afternoon and for some reason I glanced up at the blue sky. There I saw with a most intricate amazement what appeared to me to be an arrow gliding slowly high in the heavens, like a snake gliding on a field of short grass. Slowly the strange thing floated, some sort of white foam endlessly streaming behind it. I watched it go and then heard it. It was not until about a year later that I was able to understand that the strange thing I had seen was a jet airplane.

At one point I saw a number of animals grazing by in a fairly open area. I knelt down, closed my left eye, and imitated the motions of a gunman. I shouted, "Boom!" The animals paid no attention to this wild imitation of a hunter. I picked up a piece of wood and threw it at them. Only a few trotted away, but they stopped after a short distance and resumed their grazing. This had been one of my major sources of amusements, especially when I encountered some monkeys. I would stop, smile at them, and do all sorts of motions with my hands, even wave at them. However, I always had the opposite reaction when I saw an animal that I could not identify. In such instances, propelled by terror, I would flee the area with amazing speed. When I was a child, my father had frequently advised me not to run away in the face of a lion.

"You never run away in the face of a lion," he had said. "Stand still and be firm, or pretend that you are firm." But he himself had a record of having once run away from a lion unashamedly, calling out for help, although, he admitted later, the lion had shown no indication of attacking him. And once he had refused to go with the other men to hunt the lion that had been running around the area killing cattle, explaining his refusal by saying, "Why don't you leave it alone? You know it's a mighty beast, but you seem to want to recognize its might only after he has killed one of you." Since my father had had such a record for cowardice, I was not going to do as he said, but rather as he would have done if he had been in my shoes.

I came one day to a village where they had a funeral. A woman had died and it appeared she was rather prominent in the area for I saw quite a few people gathered there to attend the funeral. Actually, in these areas, mine included, one cannot measure the prominence of a person by the number of people attending his funeral. Even children from God's most humble parents can sometimes have their funerals attended by a multitude of people. This, being the first time since leaving home that I had come to a place where the inhabitants were mourning the loss of their relative and neighbor, I did not know how to conduct myself. Customs are subject to variation from one area to another, and one would do well to acknowledge them, more especially those important ones that relate to the lives of a people. But what could I do?

If it were in my area I would proceed immediately to the area where the men were digging the grave, or if I had come too late for this, I would still go to where the men were gathered. There, little by little, I would learn the full story of the deceased, his relatives, the nature of his illness, and so forth. I would help the men dig the grave and I would stay there until after the burial itself, unless I had a most urgent excuse, such as having to go and see a relative who was dying. In most cases I would even stay there for the night. If I knew the deceased reasonably well, I would be expected to stay there for several days along with all the immediate relatives of the deceased. If I were a woman, upon coming to a village where there was a funeral, I would proceed immediately to the house where the womenfolk were gathered and mourning. I would begin mourning too, regardless of whether I knew the deceased, and since the other women would, while mourning, call out the name of the deceased, I would soon pick it up and would be calling out the name too as I mourned.

After the burial and several hours later they would feed us. Depending upon the social position of the deceased in the area, a cow, more preferably a bull, would be slaughtered to feed those who would be staying there for several days following the burial.

This then was the custom to which I was accustomed, and there was no guarantee that it would be the same here. I transferred my bag from over the shoulder where I had been carrying it and held it in one hand along with the sefuliya. With my body stooped, I walked slowly past a group of men who were sitting down. I sat a few feet away from them, not knowing what to do and afraid to say something. Better, I thought, be taken for an idiot by remaining silent than be considered impolite for doing or saying something by which, unknowingly, I would be violating some of their norms.

It was already late in the afternoon. If I were home, I would have reason to stay there for the night. But here, although I was not impressed with the thought of proceeding any farther for the day if I could help it, yet I could not be sure that it was going to be an automatic condition. I waited impatiently, my imagination running all wild. Some people in some societies, I was thinking, believe that when a person dies, a baby is born to replace him. Would it not be fatal if these people here believe that the arrival of a stranger in a village where someone has died should have some connection with the death itself?

A man wearing a round-neck shirt (like a pullover) and a pair of short trousers patched on the front on both thighs, advanced toward me. My eyes were still dry, but I was wishing they were wet.

"*Mhesha?*" he finally got through to me after he had made a few attempts at this game of communication.

"Yes, stranger," I said as politely as I knew how. Perhaps I had done something wrong and they wanted to find out if it was only because I was an ignorant stranger.

"*Kwenda wapi?*" he asked. I had expected he would be telling me about who it was or when it was that the deceased had died, but he was asking me where I was going. We talked for some time, and piecemeally I was able to put the story together myself. She had recently given birth to a child . . . she had died the previous night . . . she had been buried earlier in the afternoon.

"Very terrible," I kept on saying after each of his statements. "Have mercy, Lord."

I stayed there for the night, sleeping on the verandah with others. The chilly night was breathing a rather strong wind, and in the early hours I listened to the distant beat of the drums, most likely associated with some rituals, which told me that other villages were nearby. I could hear the occasional barking of an animal, but I was all secure on that verandah in the village of mourning. Early in the morning, the wind abated, the drums silent, and the barking disappeared, I was awakened to an orchestra of birds. It was not an unfamiliar music. I had heard it every morning at home, the same beat and the same tune, and by this music the birds like the roosters, with their closer alliance with nature, could tell man himself that dawn was approaching.

I had planned to leave that day, but one of the men had revealed to me that he and his family would be going to some village lying on my route in two days. I could, if I desired, accompany them. I was not in a hurry, and moreover I would be more sure of my way and of myself if I entered a new village while in the company of one of the inhabitants. I would wait.

There were three unmarried girls in the village, and although they were dressed they had their breasts uncovered.

Of course, at home married women did not worry about covering their breasts, but not unmarried ones. My mother's advice was still fresh in mind, but all the same I would look at their youthful breasts sticking out, always taking care to cut short my stare lest my hosts misunderstand me. The girls themselves, wholly unconscious of my clandestine stare, would go about their errands without the least concern, no comparable sign of a troubled mind.

When we left two days after my arrival into that village, one of the girls was in our company. There were five of us, the man, his wife, the girl, one little boy, and myself. This was a difficult trip because now I had the almost impossible task of barring any unwarranted look at her. Of course, I had brought on this task myself. I had preferred to walk in front of the group, but the man, who talked endlessly, was walking at the back and it would have been impolite of me to walk in front while carrying on a conversation with someone all the way back. Thus of necessity I walked directly behind the women, talking with the man behind me. With an inexhaustible store of stories I soon lost myself in the talk, only to rediscover myself when we stopped to rest.

We had passed through a village where we had seen some cattle and goats, and from him I was able to learn that even in these parts, men give their in-laws cattle or goats or money in exchange for wives. I would, after all, have the same problem marrying here or at home.

Once in their home, I did not have to worry about where I was going to sleep or what I was going to eat. I was not a stranger.

In spite of the friendly welcome I had received in that village, I had a troubled sleep the first night. I dreamed I saw my brother and sister dressed up in white, and my brother in violation of known linguistic rules had spoken something to me in English, a language he knew nothing about. I saw furthermore my father and another brother, both of whom had been dead for years. My brother was naked just as I had been used to seeing him when he was alive, and my father still had his goatlike beard and his black cloth worn in the form of a toga. They were standing, facing away from me.

"Did you learn your six?" my father asked me. I said I had, and I saw them no more. Mysteriously I had found myself at Deep Bay, talking with my grandfather and my uncle. My uncle was telling me that both my brother and sister had died on the same day, but they were not yet buried because they were waiting for me.

When I got up I had a troubled mind, trying to interpret the dream. I had been told many times that if one saw a deceased relative face to face in a dream, it meant that the dreamer was himself due to die soon. I was safe according to this interpretation because both my father and brother had stood with their faces away from me. But what about the white cloths that my brother and sister were wearing? I knew that we wrap our dead in white cloths before burying them, and this seemed to tie in very well with the latter part of the dream when my uncle said that they had both died on the same day. But then, why would they be waiting for me? I did not know.

When someone was telling me in the morning that I had been talking in my sleep and that he was unable to understand what it was that I was saying, I was not very surprised. I spent that day lost in meditations. I was not so much concerned about the death of my brother and sister, of which I was already convinced, but I was worried about my mother. She had had nine children, six had died even before I left, and now with these two gone she had probably already given up on her wandering son. I began crying, and I remember one of the men, unaware that I was crying, came up to ask if I had eaten anything. I quickly wiped away the tears and said I had not.

A fortune teller had once told her that all her troubles would end when I grew up, and unfortunately she had believed him. How much, I wondered, must she regret it now?

I did not create her problems and how could I end them? It appeared that fate itself sometimes knew no justice, mercilessly taking all away from those who had little. What muscles did I have to struggle with fate itself? None, for I myself was at its mercy. This dream troubled me for such a long time that when half a year later I was informed that both my sister and brother were alive, I did not readily believe it.

I had once negotiated with a man, really, literally begged him to carry me on his bicycle. This was several days after leaving the village where I had my strange dream, and the man had found me sitting beside a small stream, tossing some pieces of tiny rocks at some butterflies. The brightfully colored insects would land on the wet ground, perhaps in an attempt to get something to eat, and the rocks from a hungry man would send them flying away.

He got off his bicycle and asked me what I was doing. Then I asked if he would give me a lift on his bike. He looked at the carrier on which rested a big bundle of something.

"See," he said, "I don't have room."

"How about there, on the frame?" I asked.

He said he could not carry me on the frame. Where would I put my bag, my sefuliya?

"I will carry the bag in my hand," I said. "The sefuliya? I will wear it on my head."

He could not see if I sat on the frame with a hat on my head.

"I will put the sefuliya in the bag," I said. I tried it, but it was too big. "Let's try it, and if you can't see the way because my hat is too high, then we can abandon the idea."

He seemed hesitant. Meanwhile I was pleading with him to be merciful. I was sincere in my intentions, and if I could help it, I would not be wasting his time. I would appreciate any help he gave me.

"Can you ride a bicycle?" he asked.

I thought he feared that I would run away with his bicycle if I knew how to ride a bicycle.

"No," I said.

"That's too bad," he said. "I was thinking that we might help each other. I carry you, and when I'm tired, you carry me."

"Oh, yes, I can ride a bicycle," I said. I had told him a lie, and it was going to be hard going to convince him of my reasons, or he would begin to doubt my intentions as well.

"Try it," he said. At least he still had enough confidence in me to allow me to demonstrate my ability to ride a bicycle while he held on to my luggage and watched me. I jumped on the bicycle, wiggled a few times, then gained full control of the machine and sped some yards before coming to a stop. He picked up my things and came running.

"Where are you going?" he asked.

"Ndala," I said.

"Ndala? But I'm going toward Tabora," he said.

I did not care, I assured him. Tabora or no Tabora I would ride with him on the bike.

We sped away, taking our turns on the way. Bicycling was much better than walking, but I would just as soon fly to Uganda if I was so financially solvent that I could afford a bicycle.

When we came to his destination, Tabora was not many miles away. Stretching my muscles as I got off the bike, I followed him to his house in response to his invitation. He was running a canteen, and I remember we spent a greater part of that evening sitting in his canteen, under the light of a kerosene lamp, his wireless playing some beautiful Tanganyika music. He was interested in politics, he said. He talked of Mr. Nyerere, whom he had seen. He talked of Mr. Kenyatta, whom he revered. In the course of his political talk he recalled the parable of the Arab and the camel to emphasize some item. I was already familiar with the parable, but I had not thought much of it. Now I could, from his talk, infer that the Arab was the African, the Camel the European, and the tent the African Continent. Maybe he had a different meaning, since I believe any person would probably draw his own meaning from a parable. Roughly, the parable runs like this:

One cold night an Arab was sleeping in his tent while his camel was standing outside.

CAMEL: Master, it's cold here. Permit me to put my nose in the tent so as to keep it warm.

ARAB: Sure.

A short time later:

CAMEL: Master, permit me to put my ears in the tent, too.

ARAB: Sure, my camel.

Another short time passed:

CAMEL: Master, is there any room for my legs, too?

ARAB: I think there is a little room for that only, my camel.

The camel put his front legs in the tent, and then turning around he said: "There is no room for the two of us here. Why don't you get out?"

The Arab went out to shiver in the cold while his camel, now boss, slept comfortably in his new domain.

Poor Arab.

I breakfasted on tea with milk and scones as his customers began to hustle in. I took a hot bath, but the image in the mirror told me that I was no longer the young boy wearing a khaki uniform, straight from the secondary school, wandering about in the village like I imagined Socrates did, or sitting down to read English at a tremendous speed in response to requests from those who simply wanted me to read English to them regardless of whether or not they understood it. My face, though still as unbearded as it was when I was born, was rugged. My eyes were bigger, my hair was clumsily curled and in need of a cut. My shirt and my shorts were soiled beyond any reasonable retrieve, and they were all shiny. But the motto on my shirt, itself in black with a blue background depicting the waters of Lake Nyasa and the rising sun from beyond the eastern shores of the same lake, was still clearly visible.

I asked him if I could wash my clothes there and he said I could. He gave me a piece of soap, a vest (T-shirt), and loaned me one of the colorful togas. There was a big pan in which I could heat the water, and there was a big white basin in which I could wash them.

"I think you'll have to soak them in hot water for a while," he said.

I soaked them in hot water as he suggested for more than an hour. In the meantime, dressed in a toga, I looked just like anybody else and amused myself watching the many people in the canteen and listening to the music emanating from his wireless.

From the strangely colored water in the basin I could tell that my friend's suggestion had worked. After changing the water I washed them and dried them by hanging them over a fence. Then I went to chat with his customers.

"I will show you," he said, "where the iron is when your clothes are dry."

"I'm not going to iron them," I said.

"No?"

"I can't iron very well," I said. "Even when I was at the secondary school, I didn't iron my things."

He thought it rather amusing that one should not iron one's clothes, but it was all a waste of time as far as I was concerned. If I could afford to wear wrinkled clothes during all my stay at the secondary school, especially the period when I began to have an interest in Miss Emma Munthali, I could certainly afford to wear wrinkled clothes here in unknown places.

I lunched on a plate of rice and a cup of tea. One can see that I was living high, very much beyond my means at the time, but this was all due to the kind hospitality of my host. He did not need anything from me, except maybe to satisfy some of his great curiosity about those questions I was able to answer on things and places of faraway countries while we sat eating crackers.

Did I have a family?

"I guess," he said after a moment of thoughtfulness, "when one wants to get ahead, he has to look like a fool."

"Why so?" I asked.

"Take your case, for example. If you were wise you would have decided to stay home and look after your family, but you went away. In the eyes of some people you are a complete fool. . . . I guess I missed my chance when I had it."

I thought of my recent dream and wondered if I was not really a complete fool to desert my family. "They have not been buried yet," the dream said, "because they are waiting for you." There was nothing I could do about it now. I was too far away from home. I could only hope that I would be forgiven.

The next morning, wearing my wrinkled but clean clothes, I was ready to leave for Tabora. He could have taken me there on his bicycle, but he was not going there, and he had other matters at home which demanded his attention. Anyway, he knew another man to whom he would lend his bicycle so he could take me to Tabora. I could not decline the offer. I waited while he went to talk to the other man. I thanked him for his hospitality, and especially for the white vest he had given me. The other man bicycled me into Tabora and left me wandering there as he left to return home.

Once in Tabora, the first thing I did was to write home. It had been months since I had done so. I wished now of course that dreams were never true, and I wrote all I could even though I knew I would not get any reply. I would even ask how they were, but what was the use? All I could have written would have been to tell them I was still alive. I was not lost, and I was doing all right.

After several days of trying to get a job without any success, I got acquainted with one Joseph Lugira, living in one of the compounds. (Actually I think he spelled his name Josef.) It was rather his sarcastic remark of "I will try . . . what?" that brought us together. After he had uttered his remark I began narrating to him its meaning, where I got it, and so on.

He was working in one of the many Indian stores. He was not married, but he was living with a little brother and they were doing their own cooking. I visited his house one evening. Two days later I was invited to live with him. I was, as one would expect, responsible for my own provisions.

He was a Moslem and we found much to talk about, he about his Allah and I about my God. Really they are one, I would say. I would cite as an example the fact that he was taught to worship Allah, I was taught to worship God through His Son, and my father was taught and brought up believing that he must worship Him in the name of his deceased relatives. I would admit my unfamiliarity with his particular kind of religion, but in mine and my father's I would be in a better position to point out some similarities.

Mine maintained that Jesus had risen from the dead and is with God. My father's maintained that his ancestors, although they had achieved no such a feat as rising from the dead and therefore were just as dead as everyone knows, were some way between God and my father. They had access to God, and indeed they performed the functions of a mediator between God and my father, and if my father was careful to flatter them with a beer party or some sacrifice of the sort, they then would bring his case directly to the attention of God since my father himself as a living man did not have any access to God. And I would say that since the three of us, Lugira, my father, and myself, were of the same kind and obviously molded by the same hands, we were really, all of us, worshiping the same deity. Only because of our three different ways of worshiping Him did He appear three. (I am not talking of the Trinity here.)

We went to a Christian Church together one morning, the only time I had been to Church since leaving home. The preacher was a European, and since the ceremony was conducted in Swahili, Lugira got more out of it than I did.

Lugira persuaded me one day that with my qualifications I would be able to find a job. To be sure, he did not know what my qualifications were. He could only guess at them by the manner with which I spoke the foreign language.

"But," he added, "you would do well to look decent when applying for a job."

"Would you say I'm not decent now?"

"With that hair," he said frankly, "I would say no."

"You know how to cut hair, don't you?"

He did, but he thought that one of his friends, a younger boy, would do a better job. He sent for his friend, who, as he had said, appeared quite dexterous. But he only appeared so, and I would not really know until after he had done his job.

He brought his razor blade and a kalowena, a comb that looks like a brush, except that it has pieces of wire sticking out of the board, normally used to make hair "lie right down."

"How do you like it cut?" he asked as he began running his kalowena on my head. The hair being so curly and having known no comb for a long time, I began to feel the pain of the wires struggling to get through the many knots. He realized he was going to need all the strength he could muster to straighten my hair.

"All of it," I said, "cut it all."

I had a mirror in my hand, and I could see his face, his teeth grinding together as the knots were being broken.

He laughed loudly and then said, "Do you realize you have lice?"

"I know," I said.

"He does?" Joseph wondered.

"Here," the barber said. "Here, come and see . . . see these eggs here (on tips of hair), see this one. . . ."

"Do you have them in your clothes, too?" Joseph asked.

"I don't think so," I said, "but if I have them on my head, it's quite possible that I may have them in my clothes, too."

He was rightly worried. Since I had lived in his home for two days, he feared he had acquired some of them. It was possible, but he found no cause to worry when later we examined his hair and his clothes.

I ran my hand over the light and not-so-smooth head. I gathered the hair (together with the lice, I should think) and for a moment thought I would bury it, but, superstitious as I am at times, it occurred to me that I would be prophesying my own death. Then I pressed the hair in my hand and tried to roll it into a ball. Carefully I placed it under a tree where, if birds did not pick it up to use for building their nests or if the wind did not blow it to strange places, it would rest while the head it once covered would be planning new routes to new lands.

After taking a cold shower and looking my best, I began the task of looking for a job. If, as I had postulated at Itigi, it was easier to get a job in a large place than a small one, I would not have much difficulty here, but as it were, the opposite was the case, of course due to several other factors.

As I had been taught, I wrote a short letter of application which I would carry on me to each office I went. Roughly the letter read like this:

To Whom It May Concern:

Sir:

I have the honor to apply for a job in your office as a clerk. . . . I am a graduate of Livingstonia Secondary School, Nyasaland. . . . Attached is the letter of recommendation from the headmaster of the same School.

Yours faithfully,
LEGSON KAYIRA

Looking for a clerical job? I did not have the slightest experience. The letter of recommendation that I was referring to here said only that I had been a student at Livingstonia and who would care about Livingstonia here? There were two difficulties surrounding my looking for such a job, but the knowledge of these did not bother me. First, even if some office had been interested in hiring me, they would have had to train me, and, second, I was looking for a temporary job, one that would run for a mere few weeks to possibly a couple of months. Granting that they would pay me while training me, which was a rather common feature in some offices in Nyasaland, it would have been quite improper to leave just as soon as I had been trained.

I walked from one office to another. I would hand my letter to whoever I found there, and in most cases they would read it and ask me a few questions, then say they were sorry they did not have any openings. In one office they joked that if I spoke Swahili as well as I spoke English, it would have been a different matter. In another office, which I learned later was that of a provincial boss of some firm, I had a different kind of experience. I knocked at the door, as rules of courtesy dictated. A deep voice bellowed, "Come in." I entered, and there seated behind the desk was a big white man. He peered at me through his glasses, lifted his big hand and pointed to the door behind me. I jumped out.

I went into stores as well, and some of them would not even read my letter. Others would say, "I don't need a clerk here."

"What do you need?" I would ask.

"Nobody."

I tore up the letter and told Joseph I was not going to try again. But I was feeding on Joseph's money all this time, and I could not leave without paying him. This was no time for pride. I began looking for any type of work, no matter how bad it was, so long as it was not dangerous. I found a job where many of us mixed cement with sand and carried bricks on a wheelbarrow to the site where a building was going up. Sometimes I went to admire the builders, who, with cigarets in their mouths, examined the rising walls and with their levels checked its straightness and correctness.

In the evening Joseph and I cleaned ourselves and went laughing and idling in the streets or visiting some of his friends in the compounds. One needed discipline, a stiff personal discipline, for without it one's purpose in life could easily go down the drain just as easily as a rock rolls down the hill.

Once I met my bicycle friend. After getting over the surprise of finding me there when he thought I was piling up mileage elsewhere, he invited me to visit him whenever I could. I did one Sunday afternoon, riding on his bicycle with the man who had come to pick me up. It was an interesting evening, talking what politics we knew under the same kerosene lamp, and consuming cups of tea with scones while the wireless blasted forth Tanganyika music interrupted occasionally by the voice of a news announcer.

To one who has taken to wandering from place to place, from country to country, and to whom meeting new faces has become a common thing and making new acquaintances a routine, a good living once established survives only until the impulse to wandering revives. And when the wandering has a purpose, pleasures acquired at any stopping place must be forfeited. They can, one hopes, be acquired just as easily at any stopping place elsewhere if one remembers how one acquired them at any given stopping place. When the need for a cement and sand mixer disappears, and when the bricks have all been wheeled to their final place, a stranded man such as I departs and strikes once more for the distant destination.

I wrote another letter home, enclosing in it a five shilling Tanganyika note which, since we live so near the Tanganyika-Nyasaland border, I was sure my mother would be able to change into our currency. This was my first fulfillment of the bargain that she and I made as one condition of my leaving home, that I would from time to time, and whenever I could, send her money to keep the family clothed and the children in school. I realized now, but too late, that if I had known I was going to stay in Tabora so long, I would have asked them to write me back, always assuming that my letters reached them, that they had survived the March disturbances, and that my dream about them was not true. If my dream were true I could not imagine what had become of my mother by now.

I began to make new plans. I would not go to Ndala after all, but would go straight to Itobo, leaving Ndala on the right. From there I would leave Tanganyika's Western Province for her Lake Province, where my goal was Mwanza.

I made a special trip back to my bicycle friend to ask for his comments on this plan. Of course, it was not the easiest or the best route, but it appeared to be the one straight to my new goal. I would have to use my gumption and be flexible with the plans. I returned to Tabora carrying a pack of crackers he had given me. Joseph was not sure that I should leave. His reasoning was probably more practical than mine. If he were I, he would have tried for another job or jobs there, and after accumulating enough money he would then go by one of the modern means of transportation. I would do the same if I were he, but although I was not in a hurry and knew it would take me a long time to achieve my goal, I always felt I was wasting my time if I stayed in one place for a very long time.

"Are you really leaving?"

"Yes, I am really leaving."

"Oh, neighbor," Christian would have said, "if you knew as much as I, I doubt not but that you would go with me."

But I would still be alone, and could he not have argued that if I knew as much as he did, he would not have doubted but that I would have stayed there or home?

As it was, I followed the railroad during the first few days, and I can still remember drinking some water at one station as the train came puffing to a halt. It was going northward, the same direction I was heading, and I could only wish I was able to afford a ride on it, or better still, to hitchhike on it! I would envy the lucky passengers, pushing their way out so as to stretch their legs. Others, with bags or baskets in hands, would struggle at the doors in an attempt to get in before the train was all filled up. No, such a huge thing would swallow all of them, people, bags and baskets, but it had no room for a penniless little schoolboy, and would never put on its brakes to pick up a hitchhiker or even to ask him, "Where are you going, fellow?"

I drank my water, and envious as I might have been, I still raised my hand, waving it excitedly at the passengers I did not know. Some would wave back, but I did not care any more than I felt they cared. They would reach their destinations sooner and merely by sitting down. I would reach my destination later and merely by counting my steps, but someday I would sit down and console myself that we both had reached our destinations, and this was all that mattered. Of course this was only self-justification for being unable to ride the train because of lack of funds. I had to please myself by extolling my situation, hence my putting the emphasis only on achieving my goal, my destination, and not on how I attained it.

The train whistled and the passengers stretching their limbs on the ground outside began rushing back to their compartments, there to entrust their fate to the iron wheels, tirelessly grinding and turning on the iron parallels. A few minutes later it was all gone, but I could still hear the puff and could see the dirty smoke curling itself upward to the endless heavens.

There was no passenger house as at Itigi, but there were a couple of shacks, which were for all practical purposes private homes belonging no doubt to railroad workers. I had been told at Itigi that there were villages or homes randomly distributed along the line where the train would stop for water. This was one of those places. I spent the night there, sleeping on the floor in one room while the owner slept in the other.

It would be a rare morning if I rose without hearing that sweet and brilliant music of the orchestra of birds. In a city maybe it would all be lost in the meaningless hubbub of men and their tools. But here in the country, even the faint music of the little tit would not be passed without being recognized and appreciated. They sang, and even as I lay on the cold floor I knew it was dawn, for the signal of it had been given and there never was any error in it.

I picked up my things, but as I considered it customary, I would not leave any place without first satisfying myself that the owners saw me leave, indeed without saying my goodbye to them and thanking them for their hospitality. I would wait until the sleepy hosts would decide, at their own discretion, that it was time they woke up. Then I would leave.

I stopped following the railroad. In some places where it was quite clear I saw the line running far away. I found nothing more discouraging than to see so far, then speculate how long it would take me to get there, and upon getting there, once more to see so far. I left the line as soon as I was able to pick up a trail. I followed the path, which crossed the line at a somewhat straight degree so that, as it were, it would not have made any real difference if I followed either one of its directions. My sense of direction in these remote places was forward, north; backward, south; left, west; and right, east. I chose left and followed it without losing myself. In such instances I kept reminding myself of the change in my direction-scale. In this particular case my forward was west, my right was north, and so forth. I would, as soon as I could, take the first north-south cross trail. Forward-north was easier to remember than the other combinations.

I sat down crying and swearing. I had knocked my big toe and the next two toes against a rock. It was my right foot again, and the nail on the big toe and one of the two affected small ones, were completely broken off. I hobbled down to the shade of a bush where I continued to cry and to swear. Then I prayed, saying that I was lost in this unknown land and asking that I be delivered into friendly hands and that I be spared the slap of losing hope as a result of any physical injury.

As I have already pointed out, this was not the first time I had knocked my toes against a rock or a stump, but certainly it was one of the major ones. I remembered that as a boy, playing with the other boys in the woods, we would whenever we had a similar injury, urinate on the fresh wounds in order to "curtail" the pain. I put my foot in position as I stood up, and quick as a wink the urine hit the three toes. I had such a momentarily exasperating pain that I flung myself to the ground, and with my eyes closed, cried loudly. The toes were still bleeding. I stood up and tried again, then I got a rope from one of the trees, and wiping away both the blood and the urine from the toes, I wrapped the rope around the injured areas in the same way one would wrap a bandage. I lay on the ground and slept.

I was awakened by a strange noise. I got up quickly and could see a deer leaping up in the air as it fled from I did not know what. Its legs would hit the bushes as they came to touch the ground, then they would be off again in the air. Leaving my things there, I went to climb a tree so I could see far and see what it was that the poor little animal was running from. I climbed higher and higher. I could not see anything, although I was able to see some huts about a mile or so ahead of me. I came down, picked up my sefuliya and the other things, and started off again. I hobbled, taking care I would not knock my toes against a rock again. I could see the blood oozing out through the ropes wrapped around the toes. I walked to the huts, but they were deserted. I looked around, even entered one of them, but they were all lifeless. The charcoals at the fireplace outside one of the huts told me that it had been some time since people lived there. Inside the hut I found a net hanging from the sooty ceiling. Cobwebs were on it. There was a plate lying on the rather rugged floor. It must have been forgotten. I picked it up, examined it, then threw it back on the floor and stepped out.

I kept going. The sun was still high, and if it were not for the bloody toes, I could have covered a large territory before retiring for the day. I decided to stop at the first habited place I entered.

I found some young boys by a stream. This was a positive sign that there were homes nearby. One of the boys was sick, for he was vomiting. I asked if there were any homes near. There were. Which way? Ahead. Where was their home? Ahead. I remembered that as a young boy myself, our folk would tell us that if strangers found us away from our home and asked us where we lived, we should point in the opposite direction. I would not care if they were cheating me, for I would still be on my course if I followed their direction—on my course for the time anyway, since I was constantly reminding myself that north was on my right.

I took off my clothes and plunged into the cold water for a bath. The tiny little fish would hurry away from my— to them—huge body. I tried to swim after them in this shallow water, but it was all sport and no serious business. I sat in the sun to dry, then wrapped some more ropes around my toes.

The boys left and I walked a little way behind them. Sure enough we came to their home; a score of houses, all displaying the same monotony of similarity. I stayed in the village for several days, sleeping with some of the boys I had found at the stream. Some of them I got to know fairly well. I would amuse the little boys whenever I got a small branch off a tree and used it to brush my teeth, which, incidentally, was one of the few times I had done so.

One sunny afternoon several weeks after leaving the village, I entered Mwanza in time to see the policemen direct traffic at the major cross sections. There was a park with a few benches planted there. I sat on one of the benches, not only to rest but also to watch and admire the dexterous policeman standing not too far away from my bench, his hands making all kinds of motions.

Some woman came and mumbled something. *"Muhesya"* (stranger) is all I could say. A man came and I told him the same thing. He pointed toward Lake Victoria, and I thought he meant that there was a steamer. He beckoned, and I followed him to a big house that looked like a warehouse. It was a rest house for steamer and railway passengers and it was free. There were many people inside. I put my things near one corner and sat there.

Late in the evening a man followed by a young good-looking woman came and sat next to me. The man could speak English, and he was waiting for the steamer, which would not be arriving for a couple of days. He was going on to Entebbe in Uganda, where he would catch a plane to Tunisia. The woman was seeing him off. Was I hungry? Yes, I was very hungry. He gave me a couple of cold dry fish. In a short time only the small bones were left.

We spent the following day together, since his steamer would not be arriving for another day. The three of us roamed the town, had lunch of rice and meat at his expense, and came back to the shore for a dip into the water, although the sign posted a short distance from us said that no swimming was allowed, most likely to save us from hungry crocodiles.

His woman friend remained there as long as he was there and left for her home when he boarded his steamer. I roamed the town alone after they left, and at night I returned to the rest house filled with people. I carried my things around with me whenever I was roaming about except my sefuliya, which I always left in the house. No wonder I lost it so quickly. I found a job washing plates in an Indian canteen along with several other people and earned enough to buy a physics book which had answers to the exercises. This would keep me occupied whenever I was not working, doing my sums and comparing my answers to the book's answers. We seldom had the same answers.

I spent both Christmas and New Year in this manner, and after saving sufficient funds for a steamer passage, I took the steamer to Port Bell in Uganda.

CHAPTER 7

Legson's Progress

ON JANUARY 19 in the year of our Lord one thousand nine hundred and sixty, I arrived in Kampala, a vast and impressive commercial city in the Protectorate of Uganda.

It was a fine morning. The sun had been in the sky for two or three hours, and the thermometers were rising. As soon as I had awakened that morning I had freed myself of the heat-infested cabin down in the basement of the steamer where we were sleeping and hurried up on the deck, where I had the pleasure of admiring the scene on the not far-off shore and enjoying the cool breeze of nature's pure breath. The steamer anchored at Port Bell, only five miles away from downtown Kampala. My heart was throbbing with anxiety now, wondering whether or not I would be able to get into the city without any traveling documents. I stepped out, and slowly walked on what I thought to be the only pier, leading to the Customs Office. "Passes, passes," I could hear men calling, as the mass of people in front of me slowly shuffled along the same pier. On the left side of the pier, two men were calling out: "Schoolboys, this way please." This was my chance, really the only chance I had. I quietly joined a small group of boys and girls called "schoolboys."

"Schoolboy," one of the men would ask as each one came to pass through the line, and each one of us would nod in agreement.

I thus arrived in Uganda, my temporary destination, but

America, my goal, was still far away, far away across land and ocean. I had told my friends at home that when I got to Uganda I would know what to do next, but now I did not know. I pulled out my map as soon as I was beyond the sight of the suspecting Customs men. With my fingers I compared the distance I had covered and the distance still to be covered. I had come that far and there was no point in turning back now, I tried to console myself. At the same time I pitied myself for having plunged into such a journey. The motto on my shirt still said "I Will Try," and I repeated the words as I had done now times without number: I Will Try. My shirt, however, was dirty, my shorts were dirty, and I was dirty. I would have to stay in Kampala longer than I had expected. I would try to get a job.

"Matoke (bananas) for sale here," a young boy was calling a short distance away. Another one, standing not far from the other, was calling out, "Sugar canes for sale here." I folded my map and after putting it back into the pocket went to the boy and bought a few bananas. Sitting down to eat my bananas, I pulled out my *Pilgrim's Progress* and opened to my favorite page. ". . . and if you will go along with me, you shall fare as I myself, for there, where I go, is enough and to spare."

I walked into the city, and while in there, I looked around for a newspaper that would probably carry some articles about Nyasaland so I could bring myself up-to-date about the affairs of that land of ours, but I was unable to find any. Realizing that I had not heard from my family since I left home and that it had been some time since I had written, I hurried to a store to buy some stationery. This done, I wrote, saying I would stay in Kampala long enough for them to write me, but that I would have to write them again as soon as I had an address. Having done this, I was now ready to look for a place where I could stay for as long as the Lord desired me to stay in that place. I knew nobody in the entire city, and everything around me was strange and confusing.

People, the way they dressed, the language they spoke, the many cars I saw in the streets, and so on, were strange to me. "These people must be rich," I said to myself. I spent that night lying on a bench on the verandah of the train depot.

After wandering some five miles on the outskirts of Kampala the following day, by some good fortune I found myself inspecting a small house that the owner, a Mr. Zake, was going to rent to me for some few shillings a month for as long as I stayed in that city. I call it a house because it had walls, a roof, and a door. The floor, besides being uneven, was rugged and dusty; the walls were partly plastered with mud and partly unplastered with anything. The roof, as I discovered later, easily yielded to rain water. There was neither a bed nor a mat. However, I was not in the least disappointed with that small house. On the contrary, I liked it, for without it I do not know where else I could have found another one. Moreover, now I could write home and wait anxiously for their reply.

It did not take long to get adjusted to my new home. The well was nearly a mile away and the landlord had provided me with a tin in which I could carry the water from the well to the house. Food was not easily obtained, but my landlord reported that there were a number of people who would be willing to give me a job in exchange for food. I would always have enough to eat, he assured me, if I worked hard.

What food would they be giving me when I worked for them? I had asked my landlord. Oh, bananas, or yams, or cassava, or sweet potatoes. I had had about all the taste there was for bananas, but so far I had been eating ripe bananas. I had been buying or getting bananas that were already ripe, and all I did was eat them. Now, in all likelihood, I would get raw bananas and prepare them myself. I would peel them in the same manner I would peel the cassava roots, and I would cook them on an open fire inside the small house. I would cook the sweet potatoes in about the same manner. I would cook all these things in a tin that Mr. Zake had lent me.

As Mr. Zake had said, it was not difficult to find work around the neighborhood. A family not far off gave me the job of weeding their cassava garden. Their arrangement of payment was, I thought, interesting, because they gave me permission to dig up as many sweet potatoes as I needed at the end of each day's work. This I would do in their other garden, and with no loss of any satisfaction. However, I did not fail to realize that the job was no more eternal than I was, but I saw no solution that would guarantee me a livelihood during the period between the termination of that job and the acquisition of another. I was satisfied with the job, and all I did at the end of each day's work was dig as many potatoes as I needed and go to the house to prepare them. One day I finished weeding the garden, and just like that I was no longer entitled to the potatoes. I would have to depend upon the four shillings I still had left from my pay at Mwanza.

During one of the days that I spent looking for a job, I had occasion to wander into the city. While there I happened to bump into the British Consul Library, which was adjacent to what I was later told was the Legislative Chambers. Now that I had discovered a library I would have to come here whenever I was free, especially since I was not permitted to borrow any books since I was not a member and since it required payment of a certain fee to be a member. I was not charged anything for reading in the library.

I found another job. A man was going to plaster his house with mud, but he wanted someone to prepare the mud for him. We used to plaster our houses that way at home, and I had done such a job at home, although I had always done it with friends. He gave me a hoe with which to dig the dirt, and a pail with which to carry water from the well to make the dirt wet. When the dirt was wet I would stamp on it to make it smooth and soft. The man was going to pay me

five shillings for the job, and only at the end of the job. I
had asked if he would pay me from day to day, and I had
hoped that if he did agree to such an arrangement, I would
take plenty of time doing the job. But since he was going
to pay me that way, I decided to do it as quickly as I could
so I could get out and look for another job.

During this time I began frequenting the British Consul
Library whenever I was free. I would walk the five miles
to the city, spend a few hours reading in the library, then go
back to the house. One February morning I was hurrying to
mail a letter home, and I had hoped I would, after attending
to the duty of my letter, stop at the library and browse a
little bit before returning to the house. On the way I was
joined by a young man, who, after failing to receive a response from me to the question he had asked me in his
language, proceeded thus:

"Haven't I seen you somewhere around here?"

"I don't know." I shrugged my shoulders and recalled
what Kaliyokha and others used to tell us about the tsotsis
in Johannesburg, that they would come up to you and talk
to you in a manner suggesting they knew you. They would
thus put you at ease, then rob you.

The persistent young man, who apparently was not much
impressed by my deliberately frowned face, proceeded with
yet another question.

"Let me see," he began, "were you not in the British
Consul Library last week?"

"I have been there several times," I said.

"Maybe that's where I saw you," he said, then added: "Is
that where you are heading now?"

I would probably go there later in the day, I told him, but
at the moment I was going to the post office. Had I been to
all the libraries in Kampala, he wanted to know. No, I was
new in Kampala, and I knew only one library, the same
library where he said he had seen me.

We walked a little way together without uttering any more words. Then he broke the silence.

"You should try the American Library, too," he said. "I think it is very nice."

"You mean there is an American Library in town?" I inquired, this time not very much interested in wishing he had kept to minding his own business. "Tell me, is there an American Library in town?"

"Yes, the United States Information Service Library," he answered. "As a matter of fact, that is where I am going right now."

Did he mind if I accompanied him, I asked. Of course not, was what he said. We would go by the post office, he suggested. No, not now, I would mail the letter some other time, possibly after my visit to the library.

I was no longer interested in going to the post office. I was only interested in going to the library, where I felt that the fact of its being operated and run by the Americans would give me a sense of being nearer to America.

"Do you see it?" he asked, pointing his finger at a building in front of us.

"Where?"

"Do you see that Indian woman standing there?"

"I see two of them."

"No, not that far. I mean that woman there, that one who is now walking toward us."

That is where the library was. As we approached it, I was able to read the inscription on the front door: The United States Information Service. We entered that big house of books and books, magazines, and newspapers, and after taking a quick glance at those stacks of books, I settled myself beside the young man on a big chair and began reading a magazine that I found lying on the table.

"You know," the young man was whispering to me, "they don't charge you anything for being a member here."

"Well," I whispered back, "it's because they don't lend

books, so they figure it's unreasonable to charge any fee for membership."

"No, they lend books. They will give you a card and you can check out books with it."

"Will you please be quieter?" a lady clerk begged us. We smiled at each other, and as we turned back to the magazines, she added, "I am sure you don't want to disturb others."

Before leaving for my home I went up to the desk and asked for a card. They handed me a form, which I filled out, and I was then assured that a card would be sent to me in the mail.

I got another job. A wealthy Muganda was having an addition built to his already big brick house. He had two bricklayers working at it, but he needed someone to mix cement with sand for them. He was going to pay me one shilling each day, and I thought I would work there for a long time, but he had made arrangements to pay the bricklayers at the end of the job, and they were anxious to finish as quickly as possible. The man himself did not speak English, but his wife did. I got to know both of them very well through his wife, and at the end of each day's work the husband gave me my shilling, and the wife gave me a bunch of bananas. Sometimes she gave me cassava roots. Moreover, they gave all three of us an hour for lunch each day, and often I would not fail to get lunch from them. Later on, the husband gave me a not-so-old short-sleeved brown shirt. I remembered one day the husband and wife were seated on chairs very near to where we were working, and in front of them were three or four sticks of sugar cane.

"Beggar!" the wife called. This was the name which for some reason they had given me. (I often wondered if they were so kind to me because they supposed me a beggar.) I was handing a block to one of the bricklayers. I placed it safely on the ground, then turned around. She pointed to one of the sugar cane sticks and motioned me to pick it up. Then

she pointed to a stool nearby and told me to sit down and
eat the sugar cane. I could not disobey orders from my em-
ployer, especially orders of this sort. I was munching the
sugar cane when she asked, "Do you have a mother?"

I swallowed the sugar cane juice that was in my mouth,
and for a moment I was confused and did not know what to
say.

"Yes," I said finally. "Yes, I have a mother."

She talked to her husband in Luganda, then turned to me
and said, "We women are unfortunate. We bear sons, we
raise them up, and then they run away from us."

It was still February and a few days after I had received
the card confirming my membership at the library. I could
check out books now. There was one lying open on the
table, left there probably by the previous reader. I picked it
up, closed it, and looked at the title, *The Enduring Lincoln*.
I sat down and began reading. I came across the sentence,
"The Whig Party was moribund." I rushed to the shelf to
look for a dictionary to look up moribund.

Instead of a dictionary I saw the volume *American Junior
Colleges*. I stopped all that I was doing or was going to do,
and losing no time I picked up the volume. With rather shaky
hands I opened it, not caring where the pages fell. They
opened to "Skagit Valley Junior College, 1001 Lawrence,
Mt. Vernon, Washington. Two year program, coeduca-
tional . . ." The volume went on to describe my future college. I copied the address.

The money I had reserved for bananas was to be greatly
reduced, for on that same day I mailed a letter to Skagit applying for a scholarship. Whether or not they were going to
accept my application, I did not know, but I was happy
because now I had found a book from which I could get as
many addresses of colleges in the United States as I wished,
and so I could apply to as many colleges as I was able to
afford the postage.

I was walking back to the house when I was joined by another young man, who, upon learning that I was from Nyasaland, told me he knew a few boys from Nyasaland who were staying in Kampala. I asked him if he would take me to their place someday. He would be willing to do so, and moreover they lived near his own home, and since that was where he was heading, he invited me to accompany him if I were not hurrying elsewhere.

"Eh, you Nyasas," my guide called as we came to a soccer field where the Nyasa boys were playing soccer with some local boys. "Eh, you Nyasas, here is a countryman of yours."

There were four of them. All except one had been living there for more than a year; one was in his fourth year. One of them was a boy named Morrison Mughogho of whom much will be said later. Did I come to work in Uganda, they asked. I was just traveling, of course.

"Nyasas like to travel," my guide said.

"Yes, we like to travel," said one of the boys and I remembered the boy at Chunya telling me, "We Nyasas have a taste for traveling."

They took me to their house and there we had a good cozy chat. We all spoke Tumbuka, for they were all from the north. They prepared some matoke and we sat down, helping ourselves to the Baganda's favorite dish.

I asked them if they had already learned to speak Luganda. It was a difficult language, they admitted, but most of them could speak it, although not fluently. I said that if people could understand what they were trying to say, then they knew the language. But they could not write it, they said. Here again, I maintained that they did not write to the Bagandas when they met them, but they spoke to them. We were still eating the matoke when one asked me:

"Did you hear that our Kamuzu (Dr. Banda) is in prison?"

"Yes."

Did I know, he asked, what they were going to do to him.

"Release him," I said.

"You think so," the other one said. "Do you know how long they have kept Kenyatta in jail now?"

"But," I tried to convince them, "Kamuzu is not convicted of any crime. He is just detained."

It was now time to leave them and go back to my house. They walked with me there so they could see the place where I was living. They were not much impressed with it, and they suggested that they would help me look for another place, to which I replied that I was quite satisfied with the place myself, but that I would be willing to move to a different place if it were cheaper, and this was a rather improbable condition.

In the meantime I finished my job at the house of the good Muganda. They did not have any other job, they said, or they would have kept me working for them. I should not, they advised, neglect to pay them a visit whenever I was in need. They could count on that, I assured them. Also, I had got fairly acquainted with a gentleman who was working in the library, and he had introduced me to a Mr. Chilombo, a Nyasa working at Makerere College. I would visit Mr. Chilombo sometimes at his house at the college, and he would show me around the campus, and often he would treat me to an honorable meal that he had zestfully prepared himself.

It was on a Tuesday morning, only two short weeks after I had sent my application to Skagit Valley College that I received a big white envelope, postmarked "Mount Vernon, Wash." with a 25¢ Lincoln stamp on. It was air mail dispatched. I opened it. I read it, and read it again, and still read it again. A Muganda boy was asking if I could give him the stamp. He could get it, I said, while still reading the letter. I had heard of America, I had read of America, I had dreamed of America, but was this letter really coming from America, the America I had heard and read and dreamed of? Was I only dreaming? I shook my head. I looked back at the letter, then at the envelope itself. It was the same letter, the same envelope postmarked Mount Vernon. Here is that magic letter for those who wish to read it and share with me the joy that I had when I read it:

> *Skagit Valley College*
> *Mount Vernon, Washington*
> *February 29, 1960*

Legson Kayira
P.O. Box 15075
Kibuye
Kampala, Uganda
B.E. Africa

Dear Mr. Kayira

We should be very happy to have you as a student here. We provide a scholarship for all foreign students. This covers all fees. We should be happy also to locate a job for you (if desired) which would take care of your board and room.

Please complete enclosed application for admission form and return to me. Keep me posted as to when you would be coming. If there is any further information you desire, please let me know.

I am sending a copy of our current catalog under separate cover (regular mail) for your information.

> *Yours sincerely*
> GEORGE HODSON
> Dean

GH/mt

Enclosure: Student Application for Admission form.

That afternoon we went to play soccer and I had a chance to meet the other Nyasa boys.

"What's the good news?" they screamed as I came into the field. This told me right away that they had heard of my good letter from Skagit. They gathered around me, demand-

ing, "Where did you get the address? Give it to us." I pulled
out the letter for them to read.

"When are you leaving? Why didn't you tell us you were
going to America?" They asked me question after question,
and I could feel a joyful pride soaring through me.

"Don't be too excited," I said. "There are lots of details I
have to go through before I can be sure of it all."

"Like getting a passport."

"It is difficult to get a passport," one said.

He had applied for a passport once, he said, but his application had been denied. From his experience he concluded that
more than likely my application would, as soon as I had sub-
mitted it, be denied. I had been aware there was difficulty in
getting a passport, but I felt that this time was as good as any
to try.

"And suppose you get the passport," one supposed, "how
on earth are you going to get to America?"

"Just as I got here."

We spent all that afternoon talking about America, and we
did not even play our game. They were interested in my
plans and they too planned to apply for scholarships at
Skagit. My visit that day won me the companionship of
Morrison Mughogho, whom I have already introduced. He
came from Nthalire, really not too far away from my own
home. Now he was going to live with me in the little house
that Mr. Zake was renting me. He was a jovial boy who not
only loved to tell stories, but also loved to sing, and he and
I would sing hours on end. He would talk of what they did
in his family. Usually he would begin his stories with a proud
reference to his father's name, Kamilazova, which literally
means "swallower of elephants." We called each other Fumu
(chief or king) and often with yane (my) added to it: Fumu
yane, my chief or my king.

I received a letter from home, the first since I had left.
Mother now realized that America was not five days away.
She complained that I was being troubled and suggested

that I return home. But Nyasaland was far away now, and it was just as difficult to walk back as it was to go forward. Moreover, I was interested in the excitement of adventures into the unknown. I did not want to abandon my plans at this stage and pitifully return home like Pliable, the man who, my *Pilgrim's Progress* told me, started along with Christian on his way to Zion and ran home after he had scrambled his way out of the slough of Despond where he had fallen. Of course I made the people at home believe that I would always come home whenever I felt that I could go no farther, but that had not been intended to be an excuse for my failure.

I applied for a passport, but since I was in East Africa, my application was forwarded to the High Commissioner in Nairobi, who in turn sent me the forms to complete. I completed the forms as directed with some minor difficulties in some parts such as my age, which I had guessed to be no less than twenty-one. I had someone measure my height with a foot rule, and without a mirror around, I had to settle for my friends' suggestion as to the color of my eyes. For recommendations, I asked that forms be sent to Mr. Petty.

Morrison and I got a job. It was similar to the one I had done earlier; that is, weeding a garden. At the end of each day's work, we dug cassava for ourselves, rather than potatoes. We could, the owner of the garden assured us, get as many cassava roots as we needed. I was going to apply my experience, and I remembered Harton Mwakikunga saying, "This is the law of survival," as I suggested this plan to Morrison: Since we would have no food when we finished weeding the garden, each time we dug cassava roots for ourselves, we should bury a portion in a hole we would dig near our house. By the time we finished our job we would have a good many roots hidden away and these would keep us going while hunting for another job. It worked.

I met a boy named Oliver. He was very impressed with my plans and said he would go with me. He was a Muganda; he was very familiar with Uganda; he knew a few local dialects, and with him I would have no trouble at all on the way, but I wanted to wait and hear from the passport people. He did not have a passport either, and like all of us there, he believed he would not get it. He suggested that if we got to Sudan, the Sudanese Government would issue us passports, and he even cited examples of boys who had done this. Since I was not sure of getting the passport I had applied for, and since he sounded very sure of getting to Sudan and there being issued passports, I agreed with him that we should leave.

We left Kampala, he carrying on his back a pack of clothes and some books, and I carrying my old bag and a thermos flask Morrison had given me. I would store water in the flask and we would drink straight from it because the cup on it had been broken and thrown away. Four days after our departure we were in a small town called Masimba, about a hundred and thirty miles north of Kampala. There I saw the first signs of trouble. Oliver could not walk straight up and his feet were swelling. I suggested we stop at Masinda until he was well and ready to resume the journey, to which he answered that he was afraid. But afraid of what?

The second night after we started out from Kampala, we had slept in a canteen near the road we were following. The manager of the canteen, perhaps meaning only to frighten us, said it was possible we would encounter cannibals.

"I don't fear animals at all," Oliver said, because I had often mentioned that I was afraid of wild animals. "I fear cannibals."

I was not particularly afraid of cannibals, and I revealed to him the fact that I thought we made a good team, with him afraid of cannibals and not animals and I afraid of animals and not cannibals.

We were sitting under the shade of a tree now in the town of Masinda. He was nodding although it was not yet noon. I was reading the Bible, and I would see him make an occasional lazy yawn. These became quite frequent. Then he broke ground thus: "I think we should return to Kampala."

"When?" I asked in a surprised tone, because I could see no reason that would compel us to return to Kampala.

"Today," he answered.

"I thought," I said, "that you said you couldn't go any farther today because your feet were swelling. How could you go to Kampala, then?"

"Take a car, of course."

"You mean you are going to hire a car to Kampala, a hundred and thirty miles away? Do you have any idea how much it would cost you?"

He was going to try for one that was already going to Kampala so he would not have to pay by mileage. But we still had a problem. I did not have any money. This, he was going to solve by paying both his fare and mine. It was not difficult finding a car that was already en route to Kampala. However, when we got to Kampala, the man charged us thirty shillings, and this apparently was beyond my friend's means at the moment, for he paid his fare and left me negotiating with the angry driver about the manner of my paying him. We agreed that I would surrender my two shirts, my blanket, and the two books to the driver, and he would keep them until such time as I had money to redeem them. This arrangement taken care of, and sooner than Morrison expected me, I came back knocking at the door.

I began the old game of job hunting. I had to get a job if I wanted to claim my things from the driver. I picked up work at a company that specialized in making bricks. In the section where I was put, I was assigned to two brick makers, and I carried a brick after it had been made to a line on the ground a few yards away where it was left to dry. Then I came back to carry another one.

This went on for hours, bending down to pick up the brick, walking straight and carefully lest I drop the precious burden, bending down to put it in the line to dry, walking back to pick up another one. At noon they let us off for thirty minutes, and since I never carried any lunch with me I would always spend the thirty minutes sitting on a stump and often running my tongue over my lips to keep them moistened.

I worked for four days and found I could never keep pace with the two brick makers. In the space of time that I picked up a brick and placed it in the line, they would make four bricks. The slower I went the higher would be their pile of new bricks. I was expected to finish lining up those bricks even if it took me into the night. I began to think of quitting, but they saved me the decision by firing me. For the four days they paid me eight shillings. This was not quite enough to enable me to reclaim my things, but when I explained the situation to the driver, he kindly received the eight shillings and gave back my things, telling me not to worry about the other seven shillings.

Morrison and I had to find jobs or we would starve to death. We went to look for work at a big farm, which we were told belonged to an Indian. On the way we met a man who appeared drunk, because we could see him sway from one side of the road to the other, singing to himself as he swayed.

"My boys," the man cried as we met, "which is better, wealth or wisdom?" as if we were modern Solomons and he God.

"Why, wisdom, of course," we answered.

"You are right, my boys," he said and threw us a shilling.

We nicknamed him Mataya, meaning one who does not

care about how he spends his money. This was a good luck sign, getting a shilling from a complete stranger.

We came to the farm. It was indeed a big farm, and was fenced all around. On the gate were these signs: PRIVATE PROPERTY. NO ADMITTANCE. Ignoring the signs we went in. There were about a dozen men inside, some feeding chickens, some sweeping, one washing a car, one eating some rice (most probably at that hour what was left of his master's lunch). One spoke English and we explained to him the reason for our coming there. We were hard workers, we assured him. We could hew trees, draw water, or wash clothes. The man looked at us and asked:

"Can you dig the garden, or feed the chickens, too? The master," he added, "does not like lazy people, you see."

"We can certainly feed chickens," I said. Several cows were wandering aimlessly out in the field, and Morrison added, "And we can milk cows, too."

There were already boys milking the cows, he said. But, however, he asked us to wait while he went to fetch his master. A few minutes later, he and the master came. The Indian was carrying in his left hand an egg. Evidently one of his chickens had just laid an egg.

"*Mutaka nini?*" (What do you want?) the Indian, with a nasty frown on his face, asked.

"*Kazi,*" Morrison answered, apparently not minding the frown.

"Job," I added.

"Job! And who told you there was a job here, you . . ." he was murmuring as he threw the egg. His egg splashed on Morrison's chest, and Morrison showed a pair of clean heels. I took off when I saw the Indian stooping to pick up a stick. I had not gone four steps when the stick zoomed and whizzed over my head, striking Morrison in front of me. I stumbled and fell down and was hardly up when the Indian had me by the neck and pushed me with such force that I found myself lying flat on the ground. "You little thieves," he had been saying as he came toward me. I stood up, crying and protesting, and made for the gate. By this time Morrison was panting safely outside.

"That was close," I said when I came to him.

"Close?" he asked as he looked at me with wet eyes.

This little incident did not discourage us. It could not. We had to find a job. If Harton had been near, he would probably have pronounced that this was the prerequisite to the law of survival. Then it dawned on us that we could fish without charge at the lake that belonged to no less a personage than His Majesty King Kabaka. The lake is situated just outside his palace, and there people went fishing, most of them, for sport. We would purchase hooks and we too would go and fish there, only not for sport.

It is ironical that sometimes those who go into something merely for the sport of it have better equipment than those going into it for a livelihood. The latter sometimes lack even elementary equipment, or if they can afford it, it is normally of the crudest kind. There we were, fishing at His Majesty's lake. The sportsmen caught a good many small fish, but being good sportsmen they tossed the little things back into the water. But with our crude hooks that we had bought at a small store for a few cents and for which we had provided our own strings and our own sticks to which we tied the strings, with our equipments it was a struggle to catch even those little things that sportsmen were playing with. Whatever we caught never returned to the lake. We took it, sang our way home, and cooked it there on our open fire. It was on one of those days when, pleased with our catch, we sang merrily on the way home that a woman who was walking in front of us stopped to listen. When we came to where she was standing, she asked us in Luganda in what strange tongue we were singing. It sounded familiar to her, she said, and that was why she had stopped. Would we follow her to her house?

When we got to her house with our fish tied to a stick,

hoping she would not trouble our conscience by begging us to give her the fish, she introduced us in Luganda to a gentleman who was seated on a chair, playing a guitar. She spoke to him in a rather rapid manner, and being ourselves very imperfect at this strange tongue, we could not follow all that she said, but judging from the expression on the face of the gentleman who by now had ceased playing his guitar, we could tell that it was something in connection with us that was being talked about. It turned out that the woman had found some similarity between the sounds we made and the funny sounds that her husband, the man now seated in the chair, used to make sometimes. Of course, she did not understand him when he made those funny sounds. He was a stranger there too. He was a Nyasa. He had left his home in Nyasaland in 1945, went to fight with the British in Burma during World War II, and upon the end of the war, settled in Uganda and married. After the wife stopped telling him where she thought we were from, the husband did indeed ask if we really were from "home," Nyasaland.

We were now talking and laughing at the table, continuing the discussion we had while the wife was preparing some food. On the table, with a small candle burning slowly and feebly, sat a big dish of cooked chicken, another dish of the almost omnipresent dish in that part of the world, matoke. There was a teapot there, too, and of course some scones. We sat there with our mouths watering as the husband called upon the blessings of the Lord, thanking Him for directing us to his house. We ate and drank and cheered, and being still of good cheer at the end, we even asked them if they would like us to give them some fish. They refused our offer, since we had only one fish. We should not hesitate to call on them whenever we were out of food, they said as we left for our own house.

Sitting around our pot of fish cooking on our open fire, we conversed thus:

"You are thin, Legson," Morrison said. "Certainly you are thinner than you were a few days ago."

"You are also getting thinner," I said.

"You are thinner than I am," he said. "Let me see your wrist." He made a circle with his thumb and other fingers around my wrist.

"See, I couldn't do that before," he said when his thumb and the other fingers met after going around my wrist.

"What can I do then," I asked, "seeing that there is no food to make me fat?"

"Maybe if we keep on fishing, and maybe with the help of our new Nyasa friend, we would get fat again," Morrison suggested.

It was getting late, for it was already the end of May. I had heard nothing further from the authorities with regard to my passport. I decided one day to try and make a survey to determine if people were friendly along the way I thought I would follow immediately after whatever decision I received from the passport people. Since I was only making a try, I followed the road so that I would not get lost but would find my way back to Kampala easily.

I took the road north. At one time a lorry belonging to the Public Works Department picked me up and by the time it dropped me off, I was fifty miles away from Kampala. I had not eaten anything that morning, not because I was fasting, but simply because there was no food in the house. I walked along the road for a little while and came to a village. I left the road there, following a good wide path for some time. The scenery reminded me very much of home, especially the maize gardens. The path took me between those gardens at times, and on both sides of the path I could see the green and fresh ears of maize. My stomach made a dull and rather rioting sound, demanding food.

The sun had already set, but for a time the moon was shining. I stopped at a village and proceeded to a house.

There were two women sitting on the verandah, and sitting in front of them I greeted them in English, "Good evening," to which they did not say anything, but kept on talking between themselves as if nobody else was there. I sat there for quite a long time, wondering what I was going to do, when, lo and behold, a man appeared. He was wearing a gownlike white dress and was apparently their husband, or at least a husband to one of them. I suppose he misunderstood my being there, thinking probably that I had come to try and establish some relationship with the two females, who still did not seem to take any real notice of my being there. He spoke first, but in a language that I did not know. I tried English, but it was all new to him. He spoke again, but I did not understand him. I finally understood him.

"*GENDA*," he screamed. "*Genda*." (Get away.)

There was no time to lose. I was on my feet, running back toward Kampala. I noticed he was following me, and so I turned toward the other houses nearby, and there I hid myself under a shrub. I could see him coming, shouting, and a few men came forward to meet him. They began talking. Evidently he was telling them about me. A white cat was rubbing itself against his legs, and I thanked God it was only a cat and not a dog. I stayed under the shrub until they dispersed, then quietly I took off, heading back to Kampala. Then I saw dark clouds low in the sky, heralding the coming of rain.

I walked a little farther and came to an old deserted house which looked like old churches I had seen at home: a building with a roof about ten feet from the ground, its walls only about four feet high, but with several pillars supporting the roof. I slept in there, leaning against the wall all night long. Then suddenly, in the midst of the dark night, I was awakened by the jolting of an earthquake, a mild one but sufficient to scare a pour soul out of his wits. With the jolting over, I sat down and resumed my sleeping, leaning against the same wall that only a short while before was trembling.

I left the room early in the morning, hoping that by the time the sun was hot I would have gone a long way, but I was wrong, for I had hardly covered more than ten miles before the sun was furiously hot, and as hungry as I was, I could not walk any farther. At one point along the way I recall jumping off the path when I saw a man running, coming toward me from the front. I stood there frightened. When he saw me, he slowed down and when he was a few yards from me, he began walking instead of running. He stopped when he came to me, looked at me for a while without saying a word. Again, as I had done to the women the previous night, I greeted him in English with a quivering smile on me, but he did not say a word. He proceeded with two or three steps, then stopped again. He turned toward me and began walking backward toward his destination with his eyes still fixed on me. Then he turned and began running again.

I resumed my walking and came to another lone house. I went there to try my luck at begging for food. I found a young man who understood English, and since he was all alone at the house, the decision of whether or not to feed me was up to him. He gave me some raw cassava roots and a sugar cane. I ate them there and waited till some time in the afternoon when the heat slackened before I left for Kampala.

It was June. There had been a good deal of correspondence between Skagit and me. I was only waiting for the decision from the passport people. I received a letter from them saying that I should send them two photographs of myself and thirty shillings. This was really promising, and a very sure sign of getting a passport. But I did not have the thirty shillings, and I did not have any picture of myself. I called upon Mr. Chilombo at the University College of Makerere to see if he could lend me forty shillings: thirty shillings for the passport and ten shillings for having my picture taken. He said he would have the money ready if I called on him the following week, and when I did, he gave me a good long lecture on why he hesitated to lend me the money. He feared I would never return it because I would not be able to earn such an amount of money. He wondered, he said, how I even managed to live as I did. Anyhow, he said he would lend me the money because I was a Nyasa, in the interest of Nyasaland. I became very annoyed by the time he was through with his lecture, and I said I would not receive his money. He reprimanded me, saying this was a very silly way to look at things; he did not mean to insult me, he was only telling me what was true: I would not find it possible to earn such a large sum of money to pay him.

I was sitting in the studios of an Indian, just opposite the Kampala General Post Office. I had in my pocket the forty shillings that Chilombo had finally loaned me. I was sitting for him to take the picture. I was wearing a white shirt, and a pair of shorts. Since it was a passport picture, there was no need for my bare feet to show. But how about my neck? Well, the photographer loaned me a necktie, and he went as far as tying it for me. I could not. I was to send the two pictures to the passport authorities, and since one of them had to be certified by a person who knew me and who also held a recognized position, I had them sent to Mr. Petty, who forwarded them to Nairobi.

It was August when I got the passport, and at the same time I got a transit visa for Sudan. Mr. Petty had sent me some money, which I used to reimburse Mr. Chilombo, pay Mr. Zake for the room he was renting me, bought a pair of black shoes and a pair of khaki shorts, and not forgetting the pledge I had made to my mother before I left, I sent my brother and sister their school fees, and also wrote them saying I was leaving Kampala.

I was ready to resume my trip now. I felt strong, after

having rested for over half a year. My plans still called for getting to either Port Alexandria or Port Said, where I hoped to get a job on a freighter to New York. The prospects of the journey and of this hope of getting a job on a freighter were frightening, but I would always assure myself with sentiments of hope and trust in the Powers above.

Accompanied by Morrison I went to see the other Nyasa boys. I thought about the fact that we the Nyasas there had already agreed upon: we were spread throughout Africa. I thought of what the wife of my wealthy Muganda had said: "We women bear sons, we raise them, and then they run away from us." I could see my mother as I saw her on that morning of October 14, and I could hear her say again: "Wherever you go I will always recognize your footprints." I was walking on grass, and this grass would never hold my footprints long enough for my mother to come and say, "I know who stood there, who walked there."

"Leaving for America?" one of the boys asked, as we were sitting down to bring ourselves up-to-date with what little news we had about Nyasaland, and above all, about Dr. Banda, who was no longer in jail but already negotiating for Nyasaland's self-government. It had been our custom to share letters from home if those letters had some politics in them.

"Who? This man? Is he going to America?" asked a local boy whom I had not met before, but who evidently was acquainted with the Nyasa boys.

"And he is walking," was the reply he got from the other boy.

"No money?" the boy inquired.

I nodded my head. He then said that I could have flown to Russia if I were going there. How did he know that? He knew of other boys, he said, who were in a similar situation, but all the same they had flown to Russia. Why did he not try to do the same himself? He was not interested. I had not forgotten what Oliver had told us. He said he knew of other boys who had gone to Sudan and had gotten their passports there. He had persuaded me to do the same, but how far did we go?

I left Kampala only a few days after receiving the passport. I was still carrying my old bag in which were still those two books. Now there were two shirts, one pair of shorts, and the thermos flask that Morrison had given me when Oliver and I attempted to go to Sudan. There was only one major change on me: I was wearing shoes. Somehow I had misplaced my map, and I had neglected to get another. With this luggage then, I would walk vigorously, hurrying up sometimes, then slowing down when I reminded myself that the journey was still very long and there was no need to hurry. I walked on a road, a good road, and on paths, paths that seemed to lead me nowhere.

"I fear cannibals," was what Oliver had said only a few months before, and I had said that I feared only animals. I might have been braver at the time I said that, because at the present I was afraid of both, and with this combined fear in me I would hurry through those paths that seemed to lead nowhere. Once in a while I would be joined by a local tribesman who happened to be traveling on the same path, but even with company I would walk miles on end without uttering a single word. The reason for this silence is simple: the lack of a common understandable language. Frequently I whistled, sometimes being unconscious of it.

When leaving Kampala, I had not neglected to buy a pound and a half of sugar, which I hoped to use in the event that food was not easy to obtain. Later on my journey during that week I was not able to get food as readily as I had done in the past. I recall a few occasions when driven almost angry by a torture of hunger, I would settle for a sip or two of water mixed with sugar which I had stored in the thermos flask.

It was a little over a week since leaving Kampala that I

came to a small town called Lira in the northern part of Uganda. Being tired and weary, I sat on a verandah of what would be called a restaurant, but I later learned that they called it a hotel. A young girl who worked in the restaurant saw me as she stepped out of the brick building. I was all dusty and dirty, and I was conscious of this, indeed I was quite aware that I was unpresentable, especially to a lady. Anyway, she asked or maybe she just said something in her dialect. Here I was again: I could not understand her and all I did was shake my head, hoping she would take it to mean I did not understand, rather than that I disagreed with her.

"You stranger?" she asked. At last I had found someone I could talk to.

"Yes, yes, I am," I said. I kept on nodding my head, and then tried to explain to her what I was doing there.

"Where sleep this night?" she asked, pronouncing the "th" much as I had done myself years before when I just began learning English, as if it were a "z."

"Here, I guess," I said, pointing my finger at the smooth cemented floor of the verandah.

"I take you to my brother. You sleep there." She pronounced "my" as if it were "ma" and both "brother" and "there" as if they had z's in them.

After her work that evening she took me to her brother's house, which was only a few minutes walk from the restaurant itself. Her brother spoke no English, and he seemed rather irritated and unfriendly, even after she explained to him that I had no place to stay that night. She went out of the house after she made the introduction, leaving us together. I began to be afraid, afraid of the man with whom I could not communicate, and at the same time I began to wonder what the girl's intentions were in bringing me to someone I could not understand and then abandoning me.

He questioned me several times, but I did to him as I had done to his sister, just smiled and shook my head to indicate my ignorance of his language. Only once he made a short quick laugh, certainly as a mockery of my ignorance. I would not like to sleep in the same room with a stranger that mocked at me. I had slept in the same rooms with people I could not understand when I was going through Tanganyika, but, at least outwardly, they appeared friendly and understanding. Under these circumstances, what could I do? I could go out and sleep either on the verandah of that restaurant or somewhere within the town. But the girl came back, accompanied by a short plump girl, who, I guessed, was twenty or possibly older. The two girls were, I thought, about the same age.

For a moment my fears and suspicions were abated. The girl said that since her brother and I could not understand each other, she and the other girl were going to sleep in the same room so she could act as an interpreter. Was she kidding? This was going to be extremely embarrassing, for the room was too small for four people to sleep with any real comfort, let alone four people of both sexes. Moreover, if her intentions were to act as our interpreter, then why bring this other girl, with whom I could not communicate? This was no time for arguments. I could either pull out quietly and take my chances outside, or stay there and wait.

She proceeded to spread the only mat in the room. Without a word, her brother stretched himself on the mat, then his sister lay beside him, then the other girl. I was sitting on my bag, confused by this strange situation. Soon it would be getting dark and there was no light in the room, and it was this fact that began to frighten me. I had a ten shillings note sewed inside the hem of the short trousers I was wearing, and I was not going to lose sight of the trousers. I dozed and she asked me why I was not lying down like the rest. I took my passport out of my pocket, put it in the bag, and lay down beside the other girl and went to sleep, using the bag as a pillow.

When I woke in the morning I sighed with relief. My

ten shillings note was there, my passport was still in the bag, and everything was in its place. The sister went out, and some minutes later she came to invite me to go and wash my face, which I did, using the hot water she had put in a big white basin outside the house. This done, she gave both her brother and myself a good breakfast of rice.

I wandered aimlessly around Lira, waiting for the afternoon when it would be sufficiently cool to permit me to resume my walking. I moved from one place to another, then back to the same places, carrying on my shoulder my bag. A young man, who said he had been watching me for some time, judged from my bag and the nature of my dress that I was a traveler. Really, I saw nothing in my dress that would distinguish me from the people in town. But he had been a traveler himself not too long before. He told briefly his travels and talked of them with nostalgia and disappointment, nostalgia because he had dreamed of going beyond the seas but was not permitted, disappointment because he was not permitted to try again. He had tried to cross the Uganda-Sudan border, but being without travel documents he was arrested even before he got to the border. How did they get him, I inquired sympathetically, as I was getting interested in his adventures and in his dream, which in a way was not far from mine. There were some clever chaps patrolling the border.

"But," he added emphatically and prophetically, indeed, courageously, "I will try again."

I had no map at the moment, having misplaced it when I was in Kampala. Consequently I inquired of him as to where I should cross the border. I had a passport and did not have to worry about "the clever chaps patrolling the border" he had been talking about. What I was after was the best shortest route to the border. Nimule. He had almost reached Nimule himself, but not quite. I would have to go through Gulu.

There was a road running between Lira and Gulu, but he

had not been to Gulu himself on that road and he could not tell me about it.

After following the road for several hours that afternoon, I branched off toward the west on a trail I hoped would take me to a village. I had passed a good many isolated houses on the road and I believed I would be able to reach a village with less difficulty than I had in Tanganyika. Indeed, I reached a village where I was welcomed without any outwardly shown resentments.

I left the village much earlier in the morning, hoping that by the time the sun was unbearably hot I would have covered a good deal of ground. It was on this day that the pair of short trousers I had brought from home, being in such a tattered condition and wholly unfit to serve their purpose, were thrown away into the forest over a thousand miles away from where they started. They had served their mission nobly and I was reluctant to part with them, but at the same time I was unwilling to carry any extra luggage, especially such a useless addition as a tattered garment.

That afternoon I saw a beautiful and frightening sight. I saw a herd of elephants a short distance away on my left. Whether or not they saw me, I cannot say. If they did, they probably did not care about so small a creature, for they acted as if nothing strange was in their sight. I saw one elephant run, but I am sure it was not running because of me. When it got to two other elephants, it stopped there. I stopped for a time, considering the possibility of another herd being across my path or very near to it. As far as I could see and hear, there was nothing, so I proceeded.

I was wandering aimlessly in a town again, this time the town of Gulu, the provincial headquarters of the northern section of Uganda. It was two days after I had left Lira. I was not very far from the Uganda-Sudan border now.

A man dressed in black trousers, white short-sleeved shirt, and a pair of brown shoes seemed always to manage to be wherever I was that afternoon. I went to a stream where I sat on a rock and soaked my feet in the running water, and I had been there for something like ten minutes when the fellow came. I thought I would stay there for as long as I care and see if he would also stay all the time. But my plans were cut short when he came and introduced himself as Mr. Lumba. As a good courtesy, I told him my full name. After some discussion, he asked me where I was going, with a "This is not my business, but if I may ask . . ." I told him. I had nothing to hide.

"America!" he screamed. "Well, what do you know? I am going there myself." Then he added, "Next year."

He was going to study some science, and his community was sending him. Why did my community not send me?

"I suppose," he said, "you have a passport."

I began to suspect he was one of the "clever chaps patrolling the border" that the boy at Lira had mentioned as being about. I showed him my passport.

He examined it for some few minutes, then said, "You look very sad in the passport. Why didn't you smile?"

He asked where I was staying and suggested that I should go and stay up at the police station if I did not have any place. It was a good place, he said, and safe. I had nothing to lose, so I went.

At the police station I was questioned by three African policemen for several minutes. They examined my papers and they even had their European boss see me. He too questioned me, asking why I was going to the United States, why I was going through Sudan in particular and no other way, who if anyone was with me, and so on. They even had me sign one of their "guest" books.

I got there at about dinnertime. I saw through the window several men in uniforms and I was told they were prisoners. They were having their dinner. In one of the rooms, there were five boys from Kenya who were detained there. They had been arrested the previous day as they were attempting to cross the border and they were awaiting their hearing in court there at Gulu. One of the policemen took me to the room and introduced me to them. I had dinner with them.

That night I slept in the police quarters. There were two policemen in the room and I slept on the floor between the two beds. They provided me with blankets, though, two thick blankets each marked with a U.P.

One of the boys had his hearing set for the following morning. The boy kept on saying he was sure they would give him "an escort" back to Kenya. I never knew what came out of it, for I was not patient to wait and hear "justice" pronounced on the poor boy.

The European gentleman called me to his office in the morning before I left. He asked me some of the questions he had asked me the previous day, and I wondered if he was not satisfied with the fact that I had a passport. He was going to a small police station right on the border, and he would be more than glad to give me a lift. I agreed. Before I left I saw Mr. Lumba dressed up in his police uniform, blowing the noon bugle, for it was already past noon when I left.

The European policeman gave me a lift in his car as he had said. His wife came along and sat in the back seat with her little baby in her lap, and the fellow and I sat in the front. I thanked him when he finally dropped me off at the border, and he was kind enough to wish me good luck.

I crossed the third border that afternoon. I was now in the Republic of Sudan. I was in the Sudanese town of Nimule, only a few miles from the border. I stayed there the whole following day because I was told I could not pass without having my passport checked by the man-in-charge there, who was at the time over in Juba. I was not in a hurry anyway. I found Nimule to be one of the most unique places. It had two stores, a dispensary, a radio-telephone, and three houses. This was all the main town. About three quarters of a mile away, there was one big brick house which I was told was a rest house. About two miles away a school was under construction. In the main town of Nimule, where all these buildings except the school were located, lived no more than ten people, including the workers and their families. The school, the dispensary, and the two stores were intended for use by the neighboring villages since Nimule was too small and would have no use for these services.

A military car pulled up near one of the houses. Two men in uniforms got out, and then a boy with a suitcase in his hand. It was the boy I had met at Lira. Evidently he had tried again, but this time he was arrested in Sudan. He smiled at me, and that was all. One of the two men was the man-in-charge of the place, the man I had been waiting for. I was shown to him by one of the men that I found there. The man who spoke no English at all kept on talking in Arabic and I was pleased that my Sudanese visa was in both Arabic and English or he would not have believed I had a visa to enter that republic.

I was thus speaking to that man through an interpreter when I was approached by another man, en route to Kampala, where he was going to spend his vacation. He was coming from Juba, and once in Juba, he advised me, I should call on his friend, his co-worker in a firm whose address he gave me. His friend's name, he said, was Andrea Taku.

There was another man, clad in a white gown and a fez, who wore a black beard on his chin that reminded me of my father's. I could not determine why he was there. He seemed to take no part in any of the daily routine at Nimule. Soon I discovered he was waiting for a bus from the Uganda section, and he was expecting two girls. Already they were overdue by several days and he had become impatient, as he did not know what had happened to them.

The bus arrived, and with it the two girls. A Uganda policeman and the girls stepped out of the bus. "Girls," he said, "we shall be going back soon."

The girls were coming from Kenya and were going to Cairo. Before leaving Kenya they had made arrangements with their friends in Cairo to meet them somewhere on the way, and the man claimed that he had been sent by the friends in Cairo to meet the girls at Nimule. But the girls had been arrested on the Sudan-Uganda border because they did not have passports. However, they outwitted the police. They told the police that they were only interested in going to Nimule for a short visit, and to convince the police of their intentions, they agreed to leave all their belongings, except a Bible, with the police. But the police were not entirely convinced because they had one of them accompany the girls.

"You are wrong," interrupted the man from Cairo. "These girls are going to Cairo with me."

He embraced the girls. It appears they knew each other already.

"And who are you?" queried the surprised policeman. "They are going back with me."

They fell into an argument. The Cairo man spoke in English, then Swahili, then Arabic, and utterly confused the policeman.

"You are a policeman in Uganda, not here," he said, holding the girls' hands. The policeman had nothing to say, but he vowed he would be back in the evening to get the girls.

One of the passengers on the bus was a young Indian. I talked to him after he had shown his passport to the man who spoke no English. I learned that his name was Mohamud. His home was in Tanganyika, and he was going to London, where he hoped to study journalism. He was not expected in London for another nine months, and he hoped that in the meanwhile he could visit the pyramids in Egypt, then go on to Lebanon, where he would finally take off for London.

He and I left Nimule together, heading for Juba one hundred and twenty odd miles away. I still had my vacuum flask and I had bought another packet of sugar at Nimule. He had a pawpaw which we ate soon after we left Nimule because it was getting bad. In the morning he was a slow

walker, and stopped every few miles to rest, but in the afternoon I could hardly keep pace with him. I would follow
with my shoes hanging on my shoulders because I found it
easier to walk without them. At one time we were lying
under the shade of a tree beside the road when a lorry came
screaming over the hill behind us. Mohamud stopped it and
asked for a lift. The driver asked if we had passports, and
then agreed to give us a lift after he was thoroughly assured
that we had the papers. The driver told us that he had shot
an elephant a few days earlier and he was carrying the meat
to his home. The lorry held big chunks of meat and two
men who were riding in the back to keep an eye on it. Once,
to show us how much of a sportsman he was, the driver
stopped the lorry when he saw two guinea fowls run across
the road in front. Boom! went his gun, and only one guinea
fowl was seen hurrying in the air, flying away to safety. The
other was added to the mighty meat of the elephant.

We were disappointed because we arrived at his home so
soon, still more than sixty miles away from Juba. It was,
moreover, late and the driver told us we would find a place
on the way where we could stay for the night. This move
on his part, especially since we had not even shown any will-
ingness to proceed after we arrived at his house, indicated
to us that he was not interested in our sleeping there. I had
hoped very much that we could stay there, because I was
tired. There were quite a few men at his home engaged in
drying the elephant meat. They had fires burning, and over
those fires they were hanging those big pieces of meat.

The driver was right. We were able to find one or two
huts after every few miles. These huts were camps for people whose duty it was to see that the road was in good repair, and they were evenly spaced so that it was possible for
one to predict accurately how many of these camps or
stations one would see before one got to Juba, knowing, of
course, the number of miles from any given camp. It was
around eight o'clock in the evening when we came to the

third camp from the driver's home. Mohamud had a wrist-watch and on the way between the time we got off the lorry and arrived at that camp, we had been timing our speed. We were walking at a rate of a little over four miles an hour. Once we went five miles in an hour, but this was accomplished because we discovered we had walked two miles in almost thirty minutes, so we spent the next thirty minutes running. Anyway, we came to this camp. Although it was about eight in the evening, it was not very dark and we could see well. There were two huts at the camp, and through the door we saw a woman sitting in front of a fire. As we approached, talking loud so our coming would not be interpreted as an attack on them, a man came out from the house.

He uttered some words and from the other hut came another man. They were both wearing loin cloths. They talked and they agreed between themselves that we would sleep in the second hut with the second man. In that hut too there was a fire burning, and the floor was all white from the ashes. He did not have a mat, and like him, we were going to sleep on the bare white floor. The other man brought us some groundnuts, and for the next thirty minutes or so we cracked them and munched. Another man, a third man, came from nowhere. He spoke Swahili and said that he would be glad to take us to his home, where he had a good house and a bed. He was not able to convince Mohamud, who was fluent in Swahili, it being his language.

"Eh," Mohamud poked me in the ribs as we were getting ready to lie down. "Do you see those?"

He was pointing at the picks and spades leaning against the wall. "I think," he suggested, "we better sleep in turns."

I was beginning to get worried. Mohamud was hungry and it appeared he could not walk very far, yet we had been on the road for only a few hours that morning after we left the camp where we had slept. There was nothing I could do. I was hungry myself. He saw some fruits about the size of white grapes which he said were similar to some of the fruits he used to eat when he was a child in India, where he was born. We gathered a heap of them but threw them away after he tasted one and found it different from those he ate in India. We came to a regular village, not a camp, where they gave us some water to drink. This kept us going for another two hours until exhausted and hungry we lay beside the road completely unsure of the next step.

Most of us have at one time or another found ourselves in a similar situation. We are desperate, we lose all hope because we neither see nor expect any help, and sometimes we are amazed by the unexpected. There we were, lying on the ground beside the dusty road. We slept. We were awakened by the driver who had given us a lift the previous day. He was driving to Juba for business and had seen us as he was passing. He gave us some cooked meat, which I have never doubted was the meat of that big animal called elephant. We ate the meat as the lorry sped through the dust to Juba, less than a score of miles away.

We crossed the Nile on a ferry and entered Juba. No sooner had we stepped off the ferry than we were in the hands of the Immigration people. They took us to their main office downtown. Mohamud was to be sent back. He had a valid passport, but he did not have a visa for Sudan. They would give him a free ride as far as the border and there he would have to take to his own means. My passport was valid, and so was my visa. How long was I going to stay in Juba? I did not know. They were going to keep the passport at their office and they would give it back on my departure.

I looked for the firm where I hoped I would meet Mr. Taku. I met him, but at first he seemed hesitant because he had some difficulties with other boys before me who had been stranded at his place.

I stayed at his house for four days, and when I left I really felt that I was leaving a friend. He drove me to the passport office, where I went to claim my passport. Then he took me to the ticket bureau, where he got me a ticket for the steamer down to Kosti.

It was a rainy evening, and I was standing in the crowded fourth class with rain water dripping from my head. I had two canned fish packets and a loaf of bread. Since the voyage was for seven days, I knew this would not last long.

Only four things of any significance happened on that tedious voyage down the Nile.

First, the second day I became acquainted with a soldier. He was escorting some convicts to Khartoum. They had their own quarters on the steamer, and since I had slept on the floor the previous night because I had been too late to be able to find a bunk in the crowded fourth class, he managed to get me a bed in the prisoners' section. But bunks were not movable! He trusted me to them for the rest of the voyage.

Second, I made two more friends on board. They were from Kenya and they had used an ingenious method of crossing the border. They bought an old bicycle and, providing rides for each other, they crossed the border with much ease. I stayed with these two boys most of the time.

Third, a certain man would come into the cabin where my bunk was, whenever the soldier was not around, and he would talk and talk. I felt sorry that I could not talk back to him due to my ignorance of his language. He had an old pair of satin type short trousers, which he wore sometimes, and sometimes he didn't and he would walk about the deck all nude. He was not alone. We were becoming friends although we were so widely separated, but our friendship was short-lived because he accidentally broke my vacuum flask. He said a good many words after he broke it, but I never understood him and I never knew whether he was explaining to me why he broke it or whether he was asking me to excuse him. Whatever it was, the flask was broken, and dependent upon it as I had been, I was unable to conceive how

I was going to make out once I was on my feet again, this time approaching the torturing heat of the desert.

Fourth, I had a surprise visit one day. I had met a student on board who was going to the American University in Lebanon. He was riding in first class and he happened to be talking to an American tourist who was also riding in first class. He told him of me, and so he came to see me on my bunk. He was a Mr. George, he said, en route to Lebanon. I could transfer, he said, to either the third or second class upon the payment of extra fare, but he was not sure of the arrangement. I could, however, get all my meals with him in their first-class dining room. This was done all the way down to Kosti, my meals being paid for by Mr. George. He was a kind gentleman and a cheerful man, although he was angry once because the officers on the steamer refused him permission to take a picture of the friend who broke my flask and the few men who were with him. Tourists were not permitted to take pictures anywhere they wanted.

CHAPTER 8

I Arrive in Khartoum

I T W A S Sunday afternoon, September 25, 1960. The sun was low, the day calm and clear. The city stood before me in a remarkable dignity. Here and there I saw buildings, some beautiful, others ugly, some big, others small, some old, others new or under construction, but all combining to give the city a peculiar beauty.

I was tired and weak and hungry. I did not know anybody in the entire city. Everywhere I looked I saw men and women, some men riding donkeys, some standing or walking; a few places here and there I saw donkeys tied to posts and braying quietly and unconcernedly. Here and there I saw men, now kneeling, now standing, murmuring their prayers to Allah. Joseph in Tabora would have been at home here. The Arabic language was as strange to me as the city itself. "What am I going to do now?" I sighed. I picked up my bag and went about the streets as if I knew already all the directions, but my whole purpose at the time was to look for a place where I could sleep.

In front of me stood an ancient building, which, in point of fact, turned out to be a hotel, and an expensive one, too. I went straight to it. As soon as I entered, an old man, looking no younger than his building, came forth to ask me:

"What do you want here?"

"I am a stranger here, sir," I trembled the words, "and I am looking for a place to stay for the night."

"This is a hotel, all right," he said in a rather friendly manner, "but I am afraid it's too expensive. I have another one in town here, and I'm sure it will suit you."

He drove me to his cheap place. It was a clean place, though no less ancient than the other. I stayed there for the night in the company of a few Egyptians, who, it appeared, were living there regularly. We slept out doors, surrounded by a brick fence, because it was hot.

The sun had just risen, bringing with it the active rushings common to all big cities. The mercury on the wall was rising, and I was sitting at a table sipping a hot cup of tea that the manager of the place had just given me. The manager, awed by my tale, was sitting opposite me with his mouth half open in amazement. On my right were two Egyptians, one of whom kept saying, "Is that so?"

The manager asked me if I needed any more tea. I did not. He then suggested that I take a good shower and gave me a piece of soap, thus reminding me of my Indian friend at Itigi more than a year before. After taking my cold shower I put on my khaki shorts, my shirt, and a pair of the soon-to-be-no-more shoes, and I can say that I looked my best, better indeed than even my own mother had been used to seeing me. I took the necessary documents and went about in town hunting for the American Embassy. I would try for a visa there, and if they refused I would go on and try again in Cairo.

For some reason, mostly language barriers, I refrained from asking others the direction to the American Embassy, but walked here and there as if aimlessly, sometimes even coming back to the streets where I had been before. Then one time, looking at a far distance, I saw with extreme delight the Stars and Stripes. The flag was waving gently.

"There it is," I shouted to myself, pointing to it as though I had suddenly become possessed. With much haste I ran over.

I took the stairway and in no time at all I was panting

before a rather bewildered lady in the office. Luckily the phone began ringing, and while she was attending to it, I regained my breath.

"Yes, sir," she said as soon as she had put the receiver back, "what can I do for you?"

"I am going to America," I breathed out. "I want a visa."

"Do you have Form 1-20?"

"What?"

"Form 1-20."

I did not have it, indeed, I did not even know what she was talking about. She began explaining to me, saying that I could not be granted a visa until I had this form, among other things. The college should have sent me that form.

"I am sorry," she said. "I can only help you if you get the form."

I was disappointed and angry. I hesitated a moment, then stood up to go. I looked at the map of the United States hanging on the wall, a row of magazines on the shelf, and back at the lady, but she had already said she could not help me until I got the form. Cairo, I was sure, would tell me the same story.

A gentleman came into the office. His name, as I later learned, was A. Salam Yausif Hamid, and he was working in the Embassy. The lady, who probably thought it was funny for someone just to come into the office and ask for a visa while not in possession of Form 1-20, began relating my case to him. It appears he did not take it as funny, for he came to me, asked me a few questions, and then asked me to wait. A few moments later I was shown into another office. It was very tidy. A map of the United States hung on one wall, and that of Africa on the other. There was the Stars and Stripes again, not too far from the desk. The gentleman behind the desk motioned me to sit down, and slowly I perched myself on the chair.

"Your name is Legson Kayira?"

"Yes, sir."

"And you want a visa."

"Yes, sir."

"Where are you from, Mr. Kayira?"

"Nyasaland."

"And to which school are you going in the United States?"

"Skagit Valley College, sir."

"Any correspondence with you from Skagit?"

"Yes, sir," I said. I unfolded two letters from my passport where I had kept them, and handed them to him. He read them through rather carefully and slowly.

"All right," he said. "How do you intend to get to America?"

"Walk to Port Said and work my way on a ship to New York," I said.

"Walk?" he asked. "How did you get here from your home?"

"Walked most of the way," I said.

He took a piece of paper and wrote something on it.

"When did you leave your home?"

"In 1958," I said.

"What time in 1958?"

"October."

He looked at the map on the wall, then he wrote something on the paper.

He went into the other office, leaving me sitting uneasily in the chair, wondering how I was ever going to get the magic Form. I waited until he, Mr. Emmett Coxson, Vice Consul of the U. S. Embassy, returned.

"Do you have any money?" he asked as soon as he sat down behind his desk.

"Five pounds, sir."

"Anything else?"

"Two shirts, a pair of short trousers, and two books."

"Any shoes?"

"These," I said, raising one foot up and pointing.

He said that it was cold in America and that he did not

see how I could expect to walk on snow with my holed shoes. I said I would, but it was because I did not know what snow was that I said so.

He glanced at the map of Africa hanging on the wall, then asked where my home was. I said it was Karonga and we looked for it, but it was not there.

"Well," he said, "you do not have Form 1-20. Also, the regulations require that an applicant for a visa should have sufficient money for a round trip ticket, and you do not have that."

Then he said that he thought it was only reasonable that I should just go back home. I did not say a word, but in my heart, "Never, no, not now."

Another gentleman came into the office. He was asking for a visa too, saying he was going to work on his Ph.D. A visa was issued him, and I looked at him enviously.

Mr. Coxson then handed me a piece of paper and a pencil, and asked me to write what I had told him. I wrote the following:

In October in the year of our Lord 1958, having completed my Junior Leaving Certificate at the Livingstonia Secondary School, I left my poor mother and a brother and a sister, the only people in the family. I walked all the way to Tanganyika. My aim of leaving the country was to go out and look for schools. There are only four secondary schools in Nyasaland and there are hundreds of boys and girls who do not find schools yearly and eventually they just stay at home. No work for them and no doubt these are the people who will soon become thieves and damage the country.

With this view in mind, I therefore left the country and embarked on a journey, a long and difficult journey, a journey to glory or death. I crossed Tanganyika, worked on the way to get some cents for food. In January this year I crossed Lake Victoria and reached Kampala. It was very difficult to find a job but I had some little money to keep me alive. I used to pass time in the libraries and happened to apply to U.S.A. On being told that I could be offered a course of study there, I applied for a passport to the Nyasaland Government. I got the passport from the Commissioner for Rhodesia and Nyasaland, P.O. Box 1612, Nairobi, Kenya. On 5th September, I traveled 50 miles then got a lift by a van to Lira. The next day I traveled to Gulu. At Gulu I stayed with police for three days waiting for a bus to Nimule. On 10th September I was at Nimule. On 13th I walked for 32 miles then got a lift by a van for 50 miles, the next day I walked for 24 miles then the same lorry picked me to Juba. In Juba I stayed with Mr. Andrea Taku, Box 51, for three days. On Sunday morning, I left Juba by boat to Kosti, a voyage of seven days. I had no food but, by the mercy of God, on the boat was an American tourist, Mr. George from Chicago. When he was told that I was on board too, he immediately called for me. I went to him and when I told him all about my adventures, he asked me to be getting food from him for the whole way up to Khartoum. I did so. On Saturday 24th I reached Kosti, the same night I left for Khartoum and arrived on Sunday afternoon, 25th September, 1960.

After I had written this, and after he had carefully read it, he wrote the following:

> *American Embassy*
> *Khartoum, Sudan*
> *September 26, 1960*

Mr. George Hodson
Dean, Skagit Valley College,
Mount Vernon, Washington

Dear Sir:

The Embassy was visited today by Mr. Legson Kayira who presented two letters from you dated February 29, 1960 and April 19, 1960 regarding his application for admission into Skagit Valley College.

Mr. Kayira has told me a story which I have no reason to doubt. Mr. Kayira's story is true—it is a classic example of a person's desire for education and, as such, warrants more than routine attention and assistance.

In short Mr. Kayira is walking and hitch hiking from his home in Karonga, Nyasaland to Skagit Valley College in Mount Vernon, Washington—approximately half way around the world. So far he has traveled the approximately 2500 miles from Nyasaland to Khartoum and so far appears undaunted by the prospect that his journey has barely begun.

Mr. Kayira's optimism notwithstanding, the Embassy is faced with the unpleasant and perhaps impossible task of discouraging Mr. Kayira from continuing on his way from Khartoum.

As you are aware certain conditions must be met before a student may be issued a visa to study in the United States. The only way that these conditions can possibly be met in Mr. Kayira's case is with the financial and moral support of your school and/or individuals in your community who may be interested in helping. I am writing this letter on the chance that someone may be interested in providing the assistance required to allow Mr. Kayira to continue on his way.

The assistance that would be required is substantial. Someone would have to undertake to guarantee his round trip passage from Khartoum to Mount Vernon and guarantee that he would not become a public charge in the U.S. I notice in your letter that the school has available a scholarship that will cover his room and board also and to provide adequate clothing. Mr. Kayira's personal possessions consist of two extra shirts and the clothes on his back plus five pounds sterling as capital.

When Mr. Kayira presented himself my first reaction was that the whole thing was out of the question and I should tell him to go back home. Perhaps this is the correct thing to do under the circumstances. After glancing at the map, however, and seeing what he has done in coming this far overseas half the continent of Africa, my conscience would not permit me to drop the affair without first satisfying myself that there is indeed no hope. Your school has indicated to him that you have some interest in him and this interest has been sufficient to impel him on a journey of unbelievable hardship with only the faintest real prospect of reaching his goal.

I shall try to induce Mr. Kayira to remain in Khartoum at least until I hear from you. In any case a visa cannot be issued without the guarantees outlined above and the Form 1-20 from your institution. Mr. Kayira tells me he wrote you before he left Kampala so I am confident you have some knowledge of his story. I am enclosing Kayira's account of his journey thus far. Your earliest reply is requested.

Very truly yours,
EMMETT M. COXSON
American Vice Consul

Mr. Coxson then asked me to check with the Embassy again in a few days.

I returned to the place where I had stayed the previous night and where I was to stay for three more days. That night, one of the Egyptian fellows took me to a restaurant. In the restaurant I sat next to a young man while my friend went to ask for a glass of Coca-Cola. Next to the young man sat another man, wearing a heavy black beard. They were arguing, and although I could not understand what they were saying since it was Arabic, I could feel that it was a heated argument. Then the young man, who gave me his name as Ayub, turned to me and asked me something in Arabic. I said in English that I did not understand Arabic, whereupon he asked where I came from. When I said Nyasaland, the bearded man looked at me in a manner suggesting that he wanted to ask me something, but he did not.

"This man," Ayub said in English, "says he speaks all the languages in Europe. I work in a German firm here, and I know a few German words, but when I ask him what they mean, he doesn't know."

I just smiled. I was not really interested in any such argument. They stopped for a while. Looking at me for the second time the bearded man asked, "*Nanga inu bambo kwanu ndikuti?*" (And you, sir, where is your home?)

I was most surprised, astounded indeed to learn that he could speak Chinyanja. Certainly he must speak all European languages.

"Nyasaland," I said again. "But, sir," I continued, "tell me, how do you come to know Chinyanja?"

"I know all major languages in Africa," he said with an obvious accent of pride. I could not doubt but that it had to be as he said.

He ordered some beer, and while waiting for his order he introduced himself as Mr. Zimba. He had studied anthropology at Moscow, where he had obtained a diploma in Chinese culture.

He bought me some bananas, and the waiter brought him his beer. I asked him where he had learned Chinyanja, but he did not answer. I finished one banana. He took his first sip of beer, then placed the glass on the table.

"What are you doing here in Khartoum?"

"I am on my way to the United States," I said.

"What are you going to do in the United States?"

"Go to college."

"I see," he said. "Why America?"

I explained to him and said that I had a scholarship.

He took another sip, then put the glass back on the table. I finished my second banana and started on my third.

"Another stooge of the imperialists," he said, lifting his glass as if to say, "A toast to a . . ."

"A stooge? What makes you think so?" I asked. I put the peels of my third banana on the table, and the waiter quietly removed them.

"I know how difficult it is to get a passport from the imperialists," he said. "You've got to be their stooge to get one, let alone get their scholarships."

"I am not getting a Government scholarship," I said.

"It doesn't make any difference," he said. "How about your passport, isn't it British?"

"It is."

"That's it right there. How did they give it to you if you weren't their stooge?"

I could not argue with him any further. I was losing my

temper, but he was quite a big man. My Egyptian friend
said it was high time we left. Ayub got himself into trouble
when he tried to help me, saying, "See, he likes to argue."

No sooner had he said this than they resumed their argument. They talked mostly in Arabic, and the Egyptian fellow would translate to me the highlights of their dispute.
When Ayub said that the bearded fellow was lying, he found
himself lying flat on the floor bleeding. The other man was
waving his fist savagely. Two men who had just entered
the restaurant were furious, accusing the waiter and the
other man of being unpatriotic to allow a foreigner to beat
one of their fellow countrymen. Mr. Zimba stood up and
walked to the door, only to be stopped by two policemen
and whizzed off.

Three days later I called at the Embassy again. I met Mr.
Hamid, who took me to a café for a cup of tea and a couple
of doughnuts, then took me back to the Embassy so I could
meet Mr. Coxson. The latter directed me to the United
States Information Agency office where I met one Mr.
Friedmann. I talked to Mr. Friedmann for some time. He
asked me to return in the afternoon, and when I did he introduced me to a tall, strong, and rather reserved gentleman. He was Mr. Harry Stuart Hudson, the Public Affairs
Officer of the Agency. He took me into his big office, where
we talked for several minutes. He pulled a one pound note
sterling from his wallet and handed it to me.

"Go pay your hotel bills," he said. "Bring your things
here and I will take you to my house where you will stay
until we hear from Skagit."

I was so amazed at his kindness that I did not know in
what terms to acknowledge it. I sat dumbfounded, staring
at him, nodding my head in agreement with whatever he
was saying, and remembering a letter that an English
friend of mine had written me when I was in Kampala to
the effect that "when you arrive in New York, you will
probably find some people willing to help you. Yanks are

very good at this sort of thing once they put it to mind."
I did not need to get to New York to prove the truth of
his words.

* That afternoon I moved to his house riding in a diplomatic car. His house was big and majestic, located in what
is called Khartoum North, on the other side of the Nile.
There was a fence around it, with two gates, the entrance
and the exit. A policeman stood at the entrance all day
and every day. The green lawn around the house could
not fail to capture one's attention, for outside the rectangu-
lar fence was sand and little grew there.

He took me into my new room, a big room with a big
window through which the morning light never failed to
penetrate. A big bed all made up already was there in front
of me. I felt afraid, then ashamed, then disappointed that
for all the years that I had also been counted among the
Lord's supreme creation, I had never dreamed let alone
thought that I would ever be of any concern as to be given
so beautiful a room and so big a bed. Pretty soon it was
time for dinner: salad, a dish of meat and rice, and dessert,
but, unfortunately for me, no bananas.

Mr. Hudson was living alone, as his family was back in
the States. In a few days I got acquainted with his cook
and his houseboy, especially the latter since he spoke English
well, and especially since I often listened to his radio. In the
morning I would sometimes ride with Mr. Hudson to town
so I could read in the Information Service library and I
would ride back with him or just walk. Later on he gave
me the job of washing the car once a week and he gave
me five shillings as pocket money. With this money I would
buy stamps and write home.

During one of those days I found three boys in the library
who, as it turned out, were from Kenya awaiting their passports. Although we had never met before, it was consoling,
mainly because we were all strangers in the city. I walked
with them to their hotel where, lo and behold, I ran into

Mr. Zimba, carrying a briefcase and still wearing his heavy black beard. Apparently the police had released him. He joined us and we walked into the lounge, more correctly, the hotel's dining room, because there were some people eating their lunches on the tables.

He asked if he could buy us something to eat. Two of the Kenya boys said they were going out for some appointment. The other boy and I accepted the offer.

While we were waiting for our order of three dishes of fried rice, Mr. Zimba told us about himself. He had lived in the Congo once, had traveled extensively throughout Europe, and so forth. I inquired if he had learned Chinyanja in the Congo. No, he had been to Nyasaland as well.

"You said you were going to America," he said. "Why are you still here?"

"Because I don't have a visa yet."

"When will you get it?"

"I don't know."

They brought our rice and we ate it without much talking, except for some little comments and laughter.

"Why did you choose to go to America?" he asked as soon as we had settled back on our chairs after the meal.

"I told you already," I said. "Where else could I go?"

"Well, there are many places. Did you try Yugoslavia?"

"Certainly not."

"That would be better for you."

"That's what you think."

"I can get you a visa in no time," he said, "and I can fly you there."

"I am sorry, sir," I said. "I have my mind on America, and I should consider it very unwise to change my plans in one minute, plans that I have been living on for two years now."

"And I should also consider it wiser to be happy later than to regret later," he said. "You don't know the Americans well. They will keep you waiting here, then at the end, when it's too late, they will say they can't give you a visa and then you will be sorry you didn't accept my offer."

"I am sorry. There are lots of students, I am sure, who can use your help."

The Kenya fellow said that he and the other boys did not know for sure where they were going. As soon as they got their passports, they would go to Egypt, where they would make further plans. I excused myself, saying that I was running for my ride home, but that I hoped to see both of them again. I was late for the ride and had to walk home. Although I had got rid of the gentleman, I had just jumped off the frying pan into the fire. On the way I was stopped by two young men. They were both studying law, they said, at the University of Khartoum.

We fell into a discussion, and when they learned that I was going to America, they began telling me about an acquaintance of theirs who had gone to the University of Chicago. It was difficult to live in America, they said.

"Have you ever heard of Little Rock?" one of them asked.

"Yes, I have," I said. Mr. Chilombo in Kampala had told me a great deal about Little Rock.

"You will have a difficult time," the other said. "You won't be able to get someone to cut your hair."

"I cut my own hair," I said. I had recently cut it, and they laughed at the erratic job I had done on my head.

"But who will wash your clothes?"

"That's no problem," I said. "I don't have any clothes that would be a problem to wash."

My transit visa was about to expire, and Mr. Hudson advised me to go to the Immigration Office and have it renewed. When I went there they told me that they did not renew transit visas. However, after I had pleaded with them for quite some time, one of the clerks asked me to go and see their boss, whose office was just behind the one in which I was. Their boss gave me some forms to complete and present them to the man I had talked to before, but when I brought my duly completed forms, they elicited the same reaction: transit visas are not extendable. I went back to the boss and explained to him the whole situation, whereupon he advised me to go to the American Embassy and ask them to give me an official letter, stating why I wanted to extend my visa and how long they thought I would remain in Khartoum. Mr. Coxson quickly wrote me that letter and I returned to the Immigration Office, but it was closed for the day, and the following day, which was Friday and their counterpart of our Sunday, it would not be open. On Saturday morning, I was waiting at the door, but when the office was open and I went in, they told me the same thing: they would not extend my visa, and this time they even told me to leave the country before my visa finally expired, which would be in two days. I did not leave the country. I lived in the country illegally.

All this time, we were waiting for word from Skagit. It was already mid-October. Often Mr. Hudson would take me for a boat ride on the Nile, or sometimes he would take me to some of his friends. I had thrown away my shoes, and for several weeks I had been walking barefoot. This was what I was used to, but it was always a fight to walk on the burning sand outside the fence. He gave me a pair of canvas shoes to wear when walking back from the library. During this time, he and I had a television interview with an American and another gentleman, who, I think, said he was from Nairobi. Also, I had an interview with a *Time* Magazine correspondent.

One morning I was waxing the floor in the house when the telephone rang. I picked up the receiver and I heard the voice of Mr. Hudson on the other end of the line.

"What was the name of your friend?"

"What friend, sir?"

"The one who wanted you to go to Yugoslavia," he said. He seemed rather irritated.

"I think he said his name was Zimba, sir."

He asked if I would spell it out for him and I did.

"There was a gentleman here a few minutes ago," he said. "He has gone to the Embassy now, I believe, and he says he is a representative from Nyasaland. He says he has met you and that he doesn't want anyone from Nyasaland to go to America."

"Would you describe him, sir?"

"He is clean-shaven. His name is Pemba." He spelled out the name for me.

This was not Zimba, I thought, because Zimba wore a beard. Pemba? I did not know anyone with that name. I took the bus and in a few minutes I was in the office. Mr. Pemba was not there. I went to the Embassy to see Mr. Coxson, and as I was climbing the stairway I met Mr. Zimba, clean-shaven now, still carrying his briefcase.

"You are not going to America," he said with a very serious face.

"I am not going to America? And who told you so?"

"Don't argue," he commanded. "See me at exactly ten o'clock tomorrow at the office of the Ministry of Foreign Affairs." He pulled out his watch as if the appointment were to be held at some hour during that same day.

"I will do that," I said.

He ran down the stairs and I ran up the stairs. I went up to Mr. Coxson's office. Mr. Coxson asked me if I knew Pemba. I knew Mr. Zimba, I said, but Zimba and Pemba were one and the same person. I should not see him again, Mr. Coxson advised. The next morning I was at the office of the Ministry of Foreign Affairs. I found the Kenya boys there, who, as it turned out, were also waiting for him. He had given them some pamphlets on economics, and he had signed his name on the pamphlets as Henry P. K. Panda. He had promised the boys some scholarship in Finland and had asked them to meet him there that morning. We waited an hour. He did not show up, so I left.

A few days later I met him again, this time in the Embassy itself, with Mr. Coxson present. What could Mr. Coxson do for him? He wanted a visa so he could attend a conference in Washington, D.C. What kind of conference? Some political conference. Mr. Coxson explained to him the regulations relating to visas. He did not seem very interested, and he left the room.

That week Mrs. Hudson arrived from the States. She was a very kind lady, and she told me as much as she could about what I would expect to find or see in America. Then one day the telephone rang. It was Mr. Hudson. He said that they had received a cable from Mr. Hodson, Dean of Skagit Valley College. The cable had said there would be help.

"Now," Mr. Hudson said, "you must begin reading about the State of Washington."

While I was reading whatever materials I could find on the State of Washington, and while Mr. and Mrs. Hudson were briefing me on the United States, Dean Hodson and Mr. Myron Mickey, the Student Body President, were forming the Legson Kayira Fund. Mr. Mickey was addressing clubs. Mr. Hodson was addressing the students and the faculty members. While I was washing a car or reading a book in Khartoum, they were staging a coffee hour at Skagit to raise funds. The Rotary Club, the Lions International, and the Kiwanis International were raising funds at their regular meetings. Churches and townsfolk in Mount Vernon and neighboring communities were responding. The Bayview Community Club was staging a dance with all the proceeds going to the Legson Kayira Fund, and they raised over three hundred dollars in one night. The radio and the local papers publicized the Fund. And so it was that the small community of Mount Vernon and the surrounding area, inhabited by kindhearted folk, raised money to help an African student stranded in Khartoum.

Mr. Robert Post of the Mount Vernon Witco Company

mailed off a ten dollar check and asked that a picture of me be taken and mailed to Mount Vernon. Mr. Mickey wrote me on behalf of the Student Body that "here in America, educational gain is unlimited." Mr. and Mrs. William Atwood and their seven children responded by offering me free room and board in their seven-bedroom home just outside Burlington. "We, as a family," they wrote me in a letter in which they had enclosed their pictures, "would like to help too, and, as such, we would be honored to have you as a member of our family."

Immediately upon receiving this most wonderful letter, I wrote the following:

> *c/o Mr. H. Hudson*
> *Public Affairs Officer*
> *American Embassy*
> *Khartoum*
> *Sudan*
> *1st November 1960*

Mr. and Mrs. William R. Atwood,

Dear Parents,

Thank you very much for your kind letter of 27th October, 1960. I shall be very glad indeed to live with you, and I am sure that my living with you will be an education by itself. By the grace of the Great Parent, I look forward to seeing you there.

As it is perhaps already known, I am a young boy of about eighteen. Our family consists of mother, myself and two others (boy and girl) both about eight years old being but twins. It is one of the poorest families that God ever created since the beginning of time; so it is little wonder that I have experienced a negative life. Such a thing is being experienced by many others in my country. I am really sorry to have put people there in such inconveniences. Surely, I am determined to be educated, so determined that I don't see anything to prevail against me save death.

I must apologize that I don't have any special tastes but I hope these will suit me. Thank you for the photos. I hope Julia will teach me some music. I think Susanne will teach me some English. Joan and Richard, I think will not be afraid of a black face in the family. But Barbara and Tommy should just be ready that when I arrive there, we shall play golf the whole night.

After all this is the meaning of life. In toil and sweat shalt one eat bread.

Excuse me, my English is very bad but I hope you will be able to follow me.

May God bless you and keep you all till we meet.

Yours very truly,

LEGSON KAYIRA

The date was November 15, 1960. The time was just a few minutes after eleven in the morning, and the sun was approaching its zenith. The sky was still as clear as it had been when I first arrived in this mother city of the Republic of Sudan, but this time the city and I were no longer strangers to each other. I had wandered to almost every corner of it, and so it was that on that day I had just returned from my wandering, and wiping the sweat off my forehead with an open palm, I entered the library, and there the librarian announced to me that Mr. Hudson wanted to see me. His office was just upstairs, and I hurried up. Judging from his smile I could guess that something was cooking.

He handed me a letter to which was attached a check for $650, which was to be used to cover the cost of my transportation. I read the letter, which was signed by Dean Hodson. I read it again, and it said that I should leave Khartoum in mid-December. I looked at the check. It looked very unreal. My lips quivered, my fingers, indeed my hands trembled, and so overjoyed was I that I felt sad and almost to the point of breaking into tears. The best I could say, indeed, the only words I could say were, "Thank you!" Two years I had wandered from strange place to strange place. Now I would wander no more.

Mr. Hudson took me to a tailor one evening to have me measured for a suit. He bought me a pair of black shoes and a suitcase. On another occasion he came into my room carrying a paper box. To my surprise, it contained nine shirts, a pair of gray trousers, two sets of underwear, one long underwear, three T-shirts, six pairs of socks, and five neckties. In just one short minute I had more clothes than all the clothes I had ever owned in my entire life. They all came from Mr. Coxson, Mr. Friedmann, and Mr. Hudson himself.

I had my medical examination and my smallpox vaccination. Form 1-20 had been sent along with the check. On the twelfth of December Mr. Coxson finally issued me a visa.

I could not leave Khartoum without having an exit visa, or whatever it is. I went to the Immigration Office. No sooner had I entered than the man who had previously refused to extend my visa, surprised at seeing me still in the city, called out:

"Didn't you leave yet?"

"I am leaving tonight," I said proudly.

"No, you won't," he said. "Your visa expired over a month ago, and you have been living here illegally."

"Well, but I couldn't leave then," I said. "This time I am really leaving the country."

"No, you aren't," he said.

"I don't understand," I said. "When I wanted to have my visa extended so I could stay here, you refused and you wanted me to quit the country. Now when I want to quit the country, you say I can't. How so?"

"You will have to pay one pound for each week that you have been here since your visa expired." He examined my visa and then said, "It will be about four pounds."

Four pounds! I would not pay it. I did not have that kind
of money.

I went back to Mr. Hudson and told him about it. He
then took me to the airport to see one of the Immigration
officers stationed there. Mr. Hudson talked to him in the
diplomatic language, and the gentleman stamped my passport thus: "Seen on Departure."

I took a warm bath, brushed my teeth, combed my hair.
Did I shave? Mr. Hudson inquired. No. He helped me put
on my first suit, a brown one, with a necktie and a new
white shirt, a pair of black shoes, and I never looked so
funny and so strange to myself, but I wished my family
could have been there to see me transformed. Mr. and
Mrs. Hudson were going to a dinner party, but he would
drive to the airport to see me off. Mr. Friedmann would
drive me there, since I would have to get there early. Parting was difficult, and after a long time of saying goodbyes,
I mumbled *paweme*, our word for goodbye.

> *I was hungry, and the Americans gave me food;*
> *I was thirsty and they gave me drink;*
> *I was naked and they clothed me;*
> *I was helpless and they helped me.*

That was on December 16. The time was eight o'clock
in the evening, a whole hour before my plane was to leave.
I jumped into Mr. Friedmann's Fairlane and was whizzed
to the Khartoum International Airport.

Some thirty minutes before departure time Mr. Hudson
arrived. A few minutes later the big BOAC jet came thundering in the dark of the night. Trembling and awed I stood
watching the lights from the big lifeless bird as it touched
the ground. I did not know what to do. I was afraid, afraid
of the thing that would take me to my destination. I was
afraid the pilot would not see the airport since we were
flying at night. We would be lost. Maybe he forgot to get
some fuel. Maybe he forgot to check his engines. There

were a thousand things to that plane. Did he check every single one of them?

I shook hands with both Hudson and Friedmann, and walked timidly to the plane. I climbed the steps and waved back at them.

"A parachute, please," I said as soon as I had been seated in the very front row of the cabin.

"Just sit down," the stewardess commanded.

The big bird roared and thundered and swung itself forward, and when I opened my eyes, which I had closed the minute the engines began thundering, I saw Khartoum lying below us as if it were only a football field seen at night, and lighted by a million candles.

III

The Journey's End

CHAPTER 9

America at Last

I WAS strolling down the long spacious corridors. I was alone. Suddenly a mysterious voice called, "Mr. Legson Kayira . . . calling Mr. Legson Kayira . . . please come to the counter." I stopped. I looked back and saw a few people way down the corridor, but they did not know me anymore than I knew them. There was nobody around me, but who was it that knew my name already? I looked around again. I was still alone. The few people down the corridor seemed unconcerned about the mysterious voice. I took a deep breath and shouted, "I am here . . . Legson Kayira, I am here." Nobody heard me. The voice stopped calling my name, and mystified as I was by the whole thing, my heart thumped violently in me. I turned and walked back to the BOAC counter. I was at New York's Idlewild International Airport.

As I walked back to the counter I could not fail to marvel at the stupendous innovations in modern transportation. Only the previous day I was lying on Mr. Hudson's green lawn, gazing lazily at the clear blue skies of Khartoum, occasionally discontinuing my gaze so as to look at a row of camels carrying their master's goods, crossing the sandy plain not far from me. Only last night an English girl returning home on furlough was helping me fasten my seat belt in my maiden plane ride. Only that morning I breakfasted on eggs in a huge restaurant at Rome International Airport and being not quite dexterous in the use of forks I spilled some on my white shirt, to the frowns of those nearby. Later that same morning I landed at London International Airport, and London welcomed her newest visitor by displaying her notoriety fog. With one of the American dollars given to me by Mr. Hudson I bought a sandwich. The lady gave my change back in American coins, and I could only take it on faith, for I was not familiar with American money.

I sat on a soft bench in the lounge, munching on my British sandwich and staring through the glass windows at the smokelike thing that was blanketing this headquarters of all of British colonialism. I turned around to the newsstand, and there, in big letters, I read of the great tragedy of the two planes that collided and crashed over New York that morning, killing some one hundred and thirty-four people. Flying to New York was no longer the thing for me. I reached into my pocket. I had only fifty-one dollars, twenty-six in bills and twenty-five in a check issued to me by Mr. Friedmann. I could not take a ship with that amount. What else? I would have to take my chance on that thing.

I was fastening my seat belt again in a Boeing 707 of the BOAC. I was becoming very expert at it now. Directly behind me a rather elegant young lady was doing the same. The stewardess, or whoever it was, announced our expected altitude and time of arrival in New York, adding that the weather forecast was poor. Already impatient, I was shaking in my seat, silently invoking the help of the Lord and the help of my ancestors who had already seen me through a continent. The big plane thundered and rolled away. Minutes later I could see the thick fog below and I knew all too well that under that thick fog the great England was still alive. Higher we climbed, and forward we went. Occasionally the white sea of clouds below us gave way to the clearly visible body of water. It was the ocean. The sun was shining, and some distance away from us, higher than us, a jet was zooming hurriedly to its destination in England or elsewhere in Europe, leaving behind it that slender stream of white vapor. Below us the ocean appeared to be all too calm whenever the clouds permitted me to see it, and I did not know whether to admire it or fear it. If the help from the Lord did not come, if my ancestors turned their backs on me, my mother would never find my bones under that clear water. I looked back at the young lady behind me and she smiled at me. I was alone, she was alone, we were all alone, united only by a machine, the plane, and whatever happened to it happened to us as well. Was she going to New York, I ventured to ask. She shook her head. She was going to Boston.

A stewardess came and sat beside me for a little chat. Where was I from?

"Oh yes, I know where Nyasaland is. It is British . . . Federation of . . ."

I almost exploded and blasted this British girl who appeared pleased at being able to recognize that Nyasaland was British. A proud smile lighted her face. An angry one flashed on mine. But this was no time to explode at anybody, especially an innocent girl whose main interest probably was flying to wherever her duty called, who never cared about how many colonies her country had.

Still wearing the same proud smile on her face she went away and came back with my lunch. Hungry for British cooking, if I may call it so, I ate merrily, despite my angry smile a moment earlier. This done, and still conscious of the plane collision I had read about, I hid my fears under the cover of sleep, no more meaningful than the giant ostrich that hides his head in sand in the face of danger.

"Sir . . ." The same girl was waking me up. I gave a deep yawn and stretched my hand to receive the papers she was handing me, for the Customs, I suppose. I completed them, and then looking through the window I saw down a row of houses, and far away I saw a big bridge. Slowly we came down and we were at Idlewild. The thermometer, it was announced, was reading twenty-eight on the ground, but it was still sunny. Without an overcoat, I ran to the building. And that is how I reached my dreamland.

I was thus running over the quick events of the day in my mind as I came back to the counter. I saw two men standing there, one carrying a machine that looked awfully complicated. They were talking to the girl at the counter, and as I approached I saw that the girl was pointing toward me. The men came forward. I had a letter in my pocket from Mr. Hudson addressed to a State Department representative who was meeting me in New York, but neither man was he. They were reporters.

That morning *Time* Magazine had put out a little story titled "Destination: Skagit Valley College." The reporters had learned from it that I was arriving that day, but I could not understand how they knew the exact time. I talked to them and then we went outside the building, where, to say the least, I was most astonished to see what I thought to be a very funny color for New York ground. It was snow, as they later explained to me. When the reporters learned that I had never seen snow before, they took a great delight in it, asking me to hold a lump of it as one of them took a picture of me with his fancy machine. It was too cold, but I was so bashful that I would not even ask them to allow me to return to the building where it was warm.

Mr. Hudson had given me some money and a picture of an overcoat from a Sears, Roebuck catalog. I was to hand these items to whoever was meeting me in New York so they could buy me a similar coat, but unfortunately nobody really met me, and moreover I was not going to spend much time in New York. In fact I did not even go into the city.

I wanted very much to see the city, ride the subway that I had heard of, and see the Empire State Building, but under the circumstances, with so limited a time, I would have to forego the opportunity. I gazed admiringly at a helicopter hovering about. I had seen two helicopters before, and ever since they had fascinated me.

Back in the building the girl at the desk showed me where I would wait for the next plane, my plane to Washington, D.C. It was getting dark, and my chances for seeing New York City were getting darker. In the lounge I met a gentleman who was working with the USIA and was a good friend of Mr. Friedmann's. He had a copy of that week's *Time* Magazine, and from my picture in it he was able to recognize me. He was flying to the Nation's Capital, and so I was in good hands.

In the air I tried to see New York through the many glaring lights, but whether what I saw was it I never knew. Soon I was in the Capital. Mr. and Mrs. Bronson Tweedy, Miss Fay Brisk of the USIA, and a few others including some reporters for the Washington *Post* and *Star* were awaiting me. I was quite tired and I must have appeared pretty dull to my interviewers. Later I was driven to the home of the Tweedys in Chevy Chase, where I stayed for the night. The mystery call in New York was now resolved. I had not been called to the counter because of the two reporters as I was led to believe as soon as I met the gentlemen. Rather, it was because Mrs. Tweedy had called the airline to check if I had arrived.

At their home I was introduced to a fascinating thing, the television. I could only shake my head at it. The program we watched featured a young teacher, a Seattle woman, if I remember correctly, who was visiting some parts of eastern Africa on a tour of duty. Another initiation was in store for me next morning. I had waffles for breakfast, but I just could not manage to put the syrup on them. Having seen neither waffles nor syrup before, I could hardly have been familiar with the sweet relationship between them. Calmly the lady of the house did it for me.

The following day I was taken to the home of Mr. and Mrs. James Byrnes, Jr., in the same neighborhood where I was to stay until I left for the State of Washington. That evening Mrs. Byrnes and I went to a cocktail party and Mrs. Byrnes watched me as I picked up a glass of whisky, vodka, or whatever the stuff was. Before I lifted it all the way to my waiting mouth, she had me by the hand. "I am afraid," she said, "you can't drink that." She handed me a glass of orange juice.

The next day, which was Sunday, was spent on an extensive tour of the city. Before we took on the tour, I had my first lecture in the United States, from Mrs. Byrnes. She taught me the different denominations of American money.

"Now," she would say, "this is one cent, or a penny, and this is a nickel, or five cents." I would repeat the words after her. Then she would assemble the coins and ask me to show her what was a dime, or a quarter, and so on. This done, we went to a department store, where she bought me a wristwatch. We then went to the home of Mr. G. Lewis Jones, of the State Department, and the gentleman gave me a heavy black overcoat which Mrs. Byrnes and the members of the family of Mr. Jones nicknamed "prime minister's coat." With this coat I was in the right mood for the biting cold. Miss Brisk, who we happened to meet again at some building where I was to talk briefly with reporters, gave me a pair of gloves, and I was ready for the grand tour of the grand city.

We left by a taxi. Our first stop was at the Lincoln Memorial. There was my hero, perpetually and nobly seated, looking too far beyond me. In a far distant land, a land he had never seen, I had heard of him, I had read of him, and I had adored his devotion to duty and his dedication to a cause. Upon hearing of his endurance, upon reading of his struggles, I had resolved to re-examine myself, rediscover myself. As he had once said that whatever he was and whatever he became, he owed to his angel mother, so perhaps the least I could say as I stood before him was that whatever I would become I owed to him. His was a mission for all of us, and our unknown future, which he sat meditating upon. Even a thunderous sound, where I to have any, would not have turned him an inch from that cause. I timidly waved at the immortal face, hoping that somehow he would see and acknowledge my mortal wave.

We rode the elevator to the top of the Washington Monument, enjoying along the way some music and a description of America's engineering feat. Once atop, and it being a not so unclear day, we were able to get a good view of the mother city of a great nation, with its different monuments dedicated to some of its greatest men. We went to the National Museum to see things from the simplest of tools and equipments to a complex missile proudly displayed outside, once again reminding us that a free man still imagines and still creates. We drove to the Smithsonian Institution to marvel at some other wonders of man's imagination.

We came back by the greatest house in the Nation, the White House. We stopped and I could only look at it from a distance, wondering if the gallant politician was in there. The flag was flapping gently atop it, assuring one that freedom still existed, that its whole future was dependent upon the man residing in that house and the people who put him there. We rode over to the Presbyterian Church where the attendant, after showing us around, stopped at the seat of President Eisenhower. He said for me to sit on it, and although I was impressively clad in my newly acquired "prime minister's coat," yet I looked too little for the seat.

All I could do was think how proud my mother would be to see her son with such humble and modest beginnings ride so high in such a great city. Little wonder that I spent part of that evening writing my first letter from America to her. Mr. Tweedy was only too pleased to mail it for me. Later that evening I met some more reporters at the home of the Byrneses.

On Monday I took another but not so extensive tour of the city. In the evening I said goodbye to my hosts and other new friends. Miss Brisk and another lady drove me to the airport, and at the airport I had one more lesson. I could not operate a water fountain. I had to turn round and round uncomfortably in an attempt to make clear my ignorance of such a common gadget.

"Do you want a drink of water?" Miss Brisk inquired. She turned the knob and, behold, there was water. She held the knob till I finished drinking.

"You better learn how to use it," she advised. "You will find these wherever you go in this country." During the remaining few minutes before my plane was scheduled to depart, I had a lecture on how to operate a water fountain, and I found the information extremely useful later on.

Once more I was fastening my seat belt. It was late in the evening and next day I would be reaching Skagit. Once we were up in the air, a lady in front of me gave me a packet of candies, which I devoured in no time. Soon I was fast asleep.

Early in the morning we landed at some airport whose name I really never knew. It was a cold morning and I paced up and down outside the small airport building, my gloved hands warmly hidden in the pockets of my heavy coat. Two military jets whistled a little distance away. One rolled down slowly, then faster and faster and soon pointed its sharp nose into the sky. It was airborne and left a clamorous thunder behind. A policeman was watching me and apparently assumed I was going to pace across the runway. He came up to me and said, "Hey, fellow, will you return to the lounge?"

It was late in the afternoon when we completed the last hop of the trip. Some two hours earlier a lady had given me three apples. I had eaten one and I was still holding the other two when we landed. After wondering what I was going to do with them, I picked up my BOAC bag and, an apology to the airline, silently "forgot" them in the plane.

As soon as I stepped out I heard someone from the ground shout, "Smile!" There were a number of people standing there, some of them looking at me through the fancy machines called cameras which I was already getting used to.

I came down, shook hands with the welcoming team from Mount Vernon, which included some students; the Atwood family; Miss Louise Helmer, one of the counselors at Skagit and one that was to be my academic adviser; Mrs. Raymond, also a counselor and a mathematics instructor. I was ushered into a building where I gave a sort of news conference. It produced the following head in one of the morning papers: LONG TREK TO GLORY OR DEATH ENDS.

The Atwoods drove me to Mount Vernon in their Buick. On the way I was given an apple which I never ate, but tossed up and down as I answered questions from a lady *Life* reporter who was riding with us.

The car came to a stop and so did the other cars in the party. I stepped out and with the others walked toward the main entrance to a big flat-roofed building. The picture of a continent, then an ocean, then another continent, flashed in my mind. It was too far away. I saw the little barefoot schoolboy saying goodbye to his mother. I saw a woman spitting on her son's face. I was far away from home, but I had reached my destination.

Mr. George Hodson, president of the College, and Mr. Neil Hamburg, president of the Student Body, were standing at the door, where a sign was displayed reading simply, WELCOME LEGSON. I shook hands with both of them amid clickings of cameras, then we proceeded to the lounge. There a group of people were awaiting my arrival. I was, so they told me later, some three hours late.

The Christmas tree was glowing in its many colors near a corner. Tables were neatly arranged, and a few uniformed girls, nursing students I learned later, were moving elegantly about. They were to serve us dinner. Meanwhile I was confronting another bevy of newsmen. Someone asked if he could take a picture of me standing beside the Christmas tree. I obliged, but I got entangled in the tree and had to be rescued by one of the Atwoods. After dinner I addressed the

party and in my unprepared speech I expressed the hope that
I would do my best so that the great help they had given
me was not given in vain. Cameras clicked and the various
reporters scribbled.

I felt most tired now. The Atwoods then drove me and
the lady reporter to their home, my new home, some ten
miles or so northwest of the college.

I was stunned to discover that Santa Claus had beaten me
to the Atwoods, indeed, that he had learned of me long before I knew him myself. I found a long stocking bearing my
name, hanging on the wall, a package under the Christmas
tree, and a bunch of letters. However, I was very tired and
I could not pay any attention to the letters. As to the package
and the stocking, of course I would have to wait till Christmas. On one of the walls hung a homemade calendar on
which the Atwood children had been marking off the days
up to the time of my arrival. I was shown into my new
room, which was spacious and beautiful.

Events were happening quite rapidly, but all I could think
of was just going to bed and resting after what was probably
my busiest day. There was one more surprise, however. Although I had talked to reporters at the Seattle-Tacoma International Airport, sitting in front of those glaring lights, I
really was not sure what some of them had done until the
Atwoods said we were going to a neighbor's house to watch
television, since theirs was out of order. I was probably
more surprised than anyone in the room to see myself on
television for the first time.

The first few days were most hectic: reading and answering some of the hundreds of letters that came, meeting some
reporters, going to the college for some orientation, constantly being reminded to speak slowly and not so much with
the hard-to-understand Scottish accent, getting acquainted
with the many admirers who came to see me.

Then it was Christmas. How different! How beautiful! I
was used only to the simple and modest manner in which we

celebrated it in my own village. No exciting preparations. Too far away for Santa Claus. No Christmas trees, no cards either. But early on Christmas morning little children ran about in the village shouting, "Christmas Box." Then families had their morning meals and cleaned themselves up. The believers, and nonbelievers if they wished, gathered together in a Church or a field. The pastor or maybe a local school teacher read the Testament, and then they gave thanks to their Maker for sacrificing His own Son to save them. The school children sang one or two carols, more often than not, "Silent Night." A dance or a football game or some other game followed and usually lasted the rest of the day.

Now it was all different and too new for me. I got up in the morning to find my stocking bulging with something inside there, more packages under the tree than there had been the previous night. After breakfast we went to the Presbyterian Church in Burlington and returned home to find that Mrs. Atwood's parents along with the Atwood's oldest daughter, Sydney, had arrived from Seattle to spend Christmas with us.

Then it was time to open presents. We had Thomas Atwood, the youngest member of the family begin the job, then it was Barbara, Richard, Joan, Susie, Julie, Sydney, myself, and so on down the line through Mr. Hamilton, Mrs. Atwood's father. Among the things I received was a Kodak from the Atwoods, which, after learning how to use, I seldom left behind. I took much delight in taking pictures of almost everything. It was more than three hours later that we finished opening our presents, and, as one would imagine, it was also time to sit down to a good dinner.

Soon it was January and I began what I had come here to do, go to college. Mr. Atwood drove me to Burlington, where he taught each morning, and there I caught the school bus to the College. As if I knew that I would make many speaking engagements later, it so happened that my first class that morning of January 2 was in speech.

During my first week at the College, I remember once anxiously waving my hand in class in response to the instructor's question and rather to the amazement of the rest of the students, standing up to give the answer after the instructor had pointed his finger at me. I was merely reflecting my previous training, for that was the proper manner in which I addressed my teachers. And I said "Sir" or "Madame," depending upon the case. Indeed, the entire class would stand up when a teacher entered the room.

Despite the fact that my schoolwork was getting heavier, there were other matters of almost equal importance that required my attention. I was taking, besides speech, beginning physics (properly, elementary physics), geometry, two courses in English, and volleyball. Although I had a good background in mathematics, mostly algebra, geometry, and arithmetic, I was not so familiar with physics, which I took as my major. This necessitated hard work on my part to keep up with the average students in the class. Volleyball was even newer to me than physics, but I caught on to it much easier.

These were not the only worries, the only things to occupy myself with. The fact that I was new in the area, coupled with the nature of my coming, was of sufficient interest so that people—more specially, clubs and organizations, particularly those clubs and organizations that had had a helping hand in bringing me here—would invite me to dinner or to address them so they could get more acquainted with me and my home. To begin with, I was not very interested in making speeches because I had never addressed any audience before, and although I had been able to talk freely and without fear to the reporters and to some few people at the Seattle-Tacoma International Airport and in the lounge of Skagit Valley College on the day of my arrival, yet I took this to be a different matter. I had dealt mostly with my own experiences, and moreover it was mostly conversation between the reporters or the people and myself.

But this time I would have to stand in front of a large number of people, clear my throat, and speak. I would try.

"That was very good," someone said as a group of people came to shake hands with me at the end of my first speech.

"At first, I couldn't understand you," another said, "but after I caught on to that Scottish drawl, I followed you pretty good."

"Do people in your home normally speak so fast?" a lady asked.

"Not so fast. Slow down," Mr. Craig, my speech instructor, would say whenever I was giving some speech in class.

After all, speaking to groups would be good practice for my speech course. In class I would learn how to slow down in my speeches, and then I would practice doing that when speaking before groups. But what about my Scottish accent?

"Just watch your r's," someone observed, "and that's all you need."

"I am not very pleased that you are already losing your good accent," my pastor at the Presbyterian Church in Burlington, who was himself Scottish, chuckled.

Within a few weeks I began to interest myself in talking to groups, speaking on my experiences, on the occupation of an average man or family in my homeland, on religion at home if I happened to be speaking before a church group, on the governmental machinery at home, but I would go this far only if I were speaking before such civic groups as the Kiwanis or the Lions or the Chamber of Commerce. At the close of my speech I would even be courageous enough to ask, "Any questions now?" And sure enough I would get them.

"Did you say you pay cows to get married?"

"How many cows do you think this woman here is worth?" they would say, teasing their wives.

"Did you say you could have more than one wife? I should go there. . . ."

Or, if it happened that I was speaking in a church, they

would ask what percentage of the population in my homeland did I think was Christian. This called for statistics and
it was hard to say for I was never sure. Or if it were at one
of the clubs cited above, they would ask if communism was
a threat to our national independence. Not that I knew of,
but if ever it were, our knowledge of its works elsewhere
would compel us to resist it.

At times I was unable to give any constructive or intelligi-
ble answers to some of the general questions. Indeed, to be
able to do so would have required my thorough acquaintance not only with the country as a whole, but also with
every problem involving all aspects pertaining to the country: history, geography, religion, economy, government, en-
tertainment, education, family relationship, and so forth. But
I was enjoying it. At one time I spoke to the Burlington
Kiwanis Club, and at the end of my speech they gave me the
highest honor by making me an honorary member. As a club
they met every Monday evening in a restaurant, and as often
as I could afford the time I attended the meetings. We would
have dinner there, and normally my dinner was all paid for.

I met again with reporters, who now were interested in
my impressions of America, how I was doing at school, what
I planned to do when I finished at Skagit Valley College.
One afternoon two gentlemen from California knocked at
our door. They had come, they said, to interview me for the
Huntley-Brinkley Report. I talked to them for two or more
hours, then they returned to their hotel in Seattle. They
would be back the following morning for the real interview,
since this one was only a preliminary.

Early the following morning, which was Sunday, they returned, bringing with them all their equipment: complex
cameras, light bulbs, and whatnot. This time they were accompanied by Mr. Charles Herring of Station KING-TV in
Seattle. I could see that it was going to be a full and busy
day.

I should add a note here of thanks to the Atwoods for their

remarkable patience. Quite often, and sometimes without any notice at all, they found themselves playing hosts to reporters. I must say they did wonderfully well.

I wore my suit bought for me by Mr. Hudson in Khartoum, and in which I had been seen on almost all important occasions since the first time I wore it. They arranged their equipment, took a few pictures, and it was time to go to church. They followed us there and took pictures as we went in and when we came out, to the delight of many folks who knew they would see themselves on television some evening.

We returned home to begin the longest television interview I ever had, certainly the longest interview of any sort I ever had. No sooner had we eaten our lunch than we started the interview, and it was not until quite late in the evening, about ten or later, that we were through for the day. They went back to Seattle. At six the next morning they returned. Mr. Atwood and I were getting ready to have our breakfast, for in a short time we would be leaving for our respective schools, he to teach in Burlington and I to be taught at Skagit. They took pictures as we munched our cereal, then followed us to Burlington, where Mr. Atwood dropped me off so I could take the schoolbus. I was on the bus, they took some pictures, then came with me to the College for two or three hours of going to class.

Although I became quite tired sitting in front of those bright lights, especially for the Sunday interview, I thoroughly enjoyed it, even the anxious moments of waiting for the telecast, which, by the way, did not come for several weeks, and then it was incredibly short.

At the College it was not all study and no play. In fact, although on the third day, in an address I had urged the students to study "with diligence and confidence," yet during those few weeks I myself was either in class or talking with students in the lounge, and seldom was I ever found in the library, except when checking out books.

I became quite friendly with two students from Seattle, Mr. Philip Campbell and Mr. John Waterworth. We were seen together often and we named ourselves, although I could not understand why at first, the Three Stooges. The TV program became one of my favorites when I discovered the source of our strange name.

I developed a great taste for hamburgers and ice cream, more especially hamburgers. The waitresses in the school cafeteria could only shake their heads when they noticed that I was able to consume three or more hamburgers a day despite the fact that I brought my lunch. No wonder that in a little over a month I soared from a mere one hundred and thirty-six pounds to one hundred and sixty.

There were many things I had to learn. A very pretty girl, Miss Pat Lee, who two months later became our Homecoming Queen, offered to give me rides home whenever I needed any, since she was living only a few miles beyond our home. I did not turn down the offer.

I remember one morning Mr. Robert Heilman and Mr. J. Closs of the Seattle *Times* came to interview me at the College. In the afternoon, Mr. Barry Farrel and Mr. Ken Harris of the Seattle *Post-Intelligencer* also came to interview me. Of course, this was after the others had left. They suggested that they drive me home so they could interview the Atwoods as well. It was approaching three o'clock, which meant I would be leaving for home in about an hour. We agreed that they would drive me home, then bring me back to the college by four so I could go back home with Pat. It sounded rather unreasonable, but they agreed.

Pat liked to dance apparently because one afternoon she was talking about how wild students were when dancing, and she thought I would probably enjoy it. Thus, at the earliest opportunity, I was at a college dance, but I danced only once, with some kind girl who had probably pitied me for just standing or sitting along the wall and came over to ask me. Those few minutes could have meant a rather nasty experience for me.

Several months later I was sitting in the lounge with a new acquaintance from Missouri.

"You remember," the student said, "the night you danced here last January?"

I nodded my head.

"I wanted to beat you."

"You wanted to do what?" I asked, very much startled.

"I wanted to beat you," he repeated. "I came here and saw you dancing. I didn't know you. Then I said to myself, 'Who is this colored guy dancing with this nice girl?'"

But we were friends now.

At the time that Pat had talked of dancing, she also mentioned skiing, and I thought this would be the next thing to try.

One morning, wearing my heavy overcoat, my pair of gloves, and several pairs of socks, and in the company of several boys, I went to Mount Baker. I rented the complete set of skiing equipment save the attire itself, and with the aid of the other boys, I managed to put them on. I could not ski. I watched some little children ski not very far from where I stood, and certainly if those children could ski, so I reasoned, I could also do it.

I gathered some courage and when one of the boys in my group was going up the hill on the chair lift, I accompanied him in my full ski outfit. When we got up there, the fellow looked around, and turning to me, he said: "That's where we are going."

I thoughtfully surveyed the area below.

"You are going there," I said, "but I am going this way." I took the chair lift back, leaving behind a skier bursting with laughter.

I have up to now said very little about my life at my new home. I would learn physics or mathematics at the College, but it was here at the house that I would also learn the other important part of my coming here, that is, to know America and Americans better. Even during the days when I felt most tired, I was never bored. I was at home, where I could smile and everybody would smile back at me and sympathize with me.

To begin with, I was given independence. I did things very much on my own, but whenever I did not know how to do something, and this was quite often, I would ask, and quite often it was Mr. Atwood who patiently explained it to me. I found him very practical. When he was home you would always see him busy, hammering on something here or doing something there.

Once he showed me how to build an electric fence around about half of their forty-acre farm to stop the cows from feeding within the area. I drove the pegs into the earth, nailed an insulator to each one of them, connected the wire, and had a fence. I felt rather proud that I had made an electric fence.

One afternoon I went to take pictures of the cows. To get to them I could have followed the wire, or I could have switched off the power and gone over it. I did neither. Instead, I decided to jump over it. I jumped but landed on the wire, and to make matters worse, it slid between my legs. I yelled and struggled to free myself and when I did, I ran back to the house without even accomplishing my task.

The children taught me games, such as Monopoly. Barbara, who was five then, taught me some little piece on piano. Once she demonstrated it to me before a large audience on television. I have forgotten the piece now.

In the evenings I used to milk a cow. I remember carrying a bucket of milk from the barn to the house, and walking beside me was Richard Atwood, who was also carrying a small bucket of milk.

"See this," he said. He swung his bucket around, but did not spill the milk. Well, here was physics in operation.

Why didn't the milk rush out as the bucket was swung up as high as his head and upside down?

"You try it," he said.

I swung the big bucket. A moment later we were both gazing at the milk, slowly disappearing under the grass and into the ground.

"I suggest," Mrs. Atwood said, "that you try with water next time."

I bought myself a bicycle and whenever the weather permitted, I cycled to school. Mr. Atwood said he would teach me how to drive a car, and I remember as we were sitting in the living room one night and talking about driving I said:

"When I know how to drive, I will drive at one hundred miles an hour."

"On whose highway?" asked Mrs. Atwood.

"That's it," snapped Mr. Atwood. "I'm not going to teach you how to drive now." That was that.

I would have to be satisfied with bicycling, for the time being anyway. But one evening when I went out for my usual evening bicycling, I passed by a house where I knew very well there was a dog that used to chase me every time I rode by. This time I approached the place at full speed, but the big dog began running after me. With all my strength I peddled along. Then the right peddle broke and the next thing I knew I was lying down a few feet ahead of my bicycle. It was at a cross section and a lady who had been waiting for me to pass before she crossed came out of her car and asked if I was all right. My knees were bleeding, my trousers torn, and my fists shaking in anger at the dog, which was now running back. She gave me a lift to the house, and once there and also as if the fault of my misadventure lay with the bicycle, I declared that I would no longer use it. I gave it to the children, who went to the trouble of repairing it.

Then Mr. Propst from Seattle sold me a motorbike for

one dollar! Very cheap. Not only was it in very good condition, but quite new, 1960 model. All my friends could
rest assured that I was not going to destroy myself with
speeding, for the thing would hardly make fifty miles an
hour. Fuel was cheap, since I averaged about one hundred
and fifty miles to a gallon. After a few hours of instructions
about running it, I was on my own.

Whereas I had spent more than five hours bicycling some
sixty miles down to Seattle once, now not only would I
ride to Seattle and back in a little over that time, but I even
drove it all the way to Portland, Oregon. There was,
however, one thing that I had neglected to do. I did not
have a driver's license to operate it, and much later I was
to stop driving it because of the same reason. The case in
question involved a car accident. A friend was giving me a
lift into town from the College one sunny afternoon and on
the way I mentioned to him that I still did not know how
to drive a car, and he offered to give me a lesson. I was
not one to refuse. We unfastened our seat belts and changed
seats in that Volkswagen of his.

"It is hard to shift gears in this car," he said, beginning
his verbal instructions. "I shall take care of the gear-shifting
and the brakes while you control the steering and the gas
pedal."

"Fine," I said.

After a few instructions we were off, with me at the
controls, and not even remembering to put on our seat belts,
a necessity which at the end I was to appreciate.

We came to a red light and he asked me to take my foot
off the gas pedal while he pushed his on the brakes. It
worked beautifully. We took off again at the command of
the green light. I could feel that we were going quite fast,
and without warning him I decided I was going to stop the
car, but I did not know where the brakes were. I stooped
down to fetch for the brakes, not aware that I could slow
down just as well if I took my foot off the gas pedal.

I heard him scream, "Oh no!" I looked up and saw that we had left the road and were heading for the Skagit River, which runs parallel to the road.

Quick as a wink I turned and came back to the road, but apparently I had turned fast and we crossed the road just as fast. A utility pole stood directly ahead of me. We both had the steering wheel, and we turned and swayed toward the road, missing the pole by inches. The car refused to go back to the road, and tumbled and began rolling. My door broke and flew off. I followed suit and landed on a pile of sand, and the next thing I knew I was hearing the noise of the rolling car. Thinking that it was rolling towards me and that any moment it would be upon me, I stood up quickly in an attempt to run away before it squeezed me. When I stood up, I found that my friend was already up. Evidently he had also come out through my door because we found out later that his had been jammed shut. I spit out sand and reached into my pockets to scoop out pieces of glass from the broken windows and doors. We were both unhurt, but the car was a total wreck.

"Who was driving?" asked one of the two policemen who arrived at the scene only minutes after the accident.

"Me, sir," I answered timidly.

"Are you all right?"

I nodded my head. The other boy nodded his. We were both all right.

He looked at the wreckage.

"Boy, oh boy," the other policeman shook his head. "When you do things you really do big ones, don't you?"

I was silent.

"May I see your driver's license?"

"I don't have it, sir."

"Did you leave it at home?"

"No sir . . . I mean I don't have any."

"Your car?"

"No, it's mine," said the other boy.

"May I see your license?"

He pulled out the license from his wallet. The policeman examined it and said:

"I am afraid you need to renew it."

He asked if I had a driver's permit. I did not. It had expired several months ago.

I wiped the dust off my face and scratched the sand from my head. I did not have any permit to drive a car. What would the Atwoods say about it? What would I tell people? I did not know.

"How fast were you going?"

"I don't know," I said.

"Guess," he said. "Approximately how fast?"

"I don't think I can even hazard a guess, sir."

"I would say thirty-five," the other boy said. "Thirty-five to forty."

"Roll a car at thirty-five miles?" the officer inquired rather doubtfully.

The other boy courageously asked how much the officer thought it would cost to fix the damaged car.

"Fix it? Well, I should think it would be cheaper just to buy another one."

It was. The tires were badly damaged, the top of the car curved inward, the glasses were broken, one door was completely smashed, the other dented and jammed. Only the glass in the back window was unbroken, though it had popped out very neatly.

By a wild coincidence, this was the same boy who had once said to me atop the snow-covered mountain, "That's where we are going."

A week later I received a letter in the mail saying that my hearing had been set for Tuesday of the following week at one o'clock, that if I preferred I could post bail of ten dollars, but that if I failed to show up at the hearing or failed to post bail, a warrant would be signed for my arrest. I posted bail in no time at all.

I thought it was high time I got a license to drive my motorbike, and so one afternoon I drove it to the state patrol office. One of the officers was watching me as I parked it.

"Can I help you?" he asked as I entered.

"Yes," I said, very confident of myself. "I want a driver's license."

"A driver's license?" he repeated. "What for?"

"So I can drive my bike."

"But you are driving it," he said. "Did you drive it here without a license?"

I nodded with a faint smile. I was not sure that I had to have a license to drive a motorbike. They would only give me a driving permit now, then test me later.

"No," I said. "I know how to drive it already, and all I want now is a license. You can give me the examinations right now."

No. They could give me a license if I knew how to drive a car. Meanwhile they could give me a driving permit to learn how to drive an automobile, and if I passed the examinations, they would give me a license and I could use it for driving either an automobile or a motorbike. The recent experience with the car was still fresh in my mind, and I did not have any interest at all in learning how to drive one.

So far in this chapter I have not mentioned a thing about my mother or my family. As I have said elsewhere in this work, my mother could not read or write, and I had to depend very much upon indirect information from friends or relatives at home. She was, my informants wrote, saying that she now thought I had come here to stay, that I would never go back, and that she was not going to let my brother and sister go to high school when they were ready because they too would run away to college and leave her alone. I should write her, assuring her repeatedly that I had no such intentions.

Then someone wrote that she was having financial problems. She needed someone to till her garden; she needed someone to repair the house; the children needed money for school fees and clothes. I sent her some money through Mr. Petty, who was still at Livingstonia, and he was going to act as her banker, sending her money as she needed it for clothes and blankets.

I received another letter from a friend who was a student at a school over a hundred miles away from home. In his letter he said simply, "I left home four days ago, and about an hour before I left, your mother was bitten by a snake. I am sorry but I don't know any further details."

From the date of his letter I knew it had been sixteen days since she had been bitten, and since my writers in the village always sent their letters by surface mail, it would be over two months before I knew anything. It was on Friday when I received the letter and I thought I would try to telephone Mr. Russell, my headmaster at Livingstonia, and ask him to drive to my village the following morning to see how she was, if she was still there, and either call me back the same day or let me call him back.

I picked up the receiver, dialed the operator, and told her I was calling Nyasaland. A few moments later some other operator somewhere was telling me to call back in seven hours. Seven long hours passed with great anxiety and expectations. It was two o'clock in the morning when I was to call back. I tried again, and the operator, anticipating it would take a long time for the call to get through, suggested that I hang up. She would call my home and then call me if anything came up. It was, I believe, more than thirty minutes later when she called to say she could not get anybody, that somebody had told her there wasn't any telephone service at Livingstonia. What to do? Early the next morning I went to Western Union to send a telegram to Mr. Russell:

INFORMED MOTHER BITTEN BY SNAKE STOP NO FURTHER DETAILS STOP PLEASE SEE HER STOP REPORT TO ME IMMEDIATELY STOP WILL PAY ALL THE COSTS STOP.

Next Monday afternoon I was at the College. Someone asked me to go to the main desk to answer a call from Western Union, something about a telegram. I was trembling. This was the time when I would know whether I still had a mother or not.

"Hello, this is Legson," I said with a surprisingly calm voice.

"Yes, Legson," the voice on the other end of the line said. He sounded calm. Maybe it was good news. Maybe he was only trying to calm me. "I have a telegram for you from Mr. John Russell. Would you like me to read it to you?"

"Yes, please."

"What did he say?" someone asked.

I did not answer. I was shaking violently. There was a moment of silence on the other end. I could hear a noise like the unfolding of a paper.

"Telegram received," he began to read. "Will do as requested. Report to you immediately. . . ."

"He said," I began to answer as I put the receiver back, "that he (my ex-teacher) would report later. Evidently he has not yet seen her."

One week passed. No news. During that time I sent four letters to friends at home, appealing to them to write me by airmail about my mother's condition.

Two weeks passed and still no news. I was so worried. I would dream at night of being home, but not seeing my mother. Sometimes I would dream of going home, meeting someone on the way who would tell me that he saw my mother leave the village on some errand and that it would be sometime before she returned. Sometimes I dreamed of getting home and seeing a woman who did not look like my mother. As soon as I came in, someone would say to her, "Your son has come back." And sometimes I would wake up just at the time when I reached home. I remembered the dream I had when my father died, and I was most afraid of having a similar dream at this time. My worries were now mostly about my brother and sister, because I could think of no one to whom I could entrust their care if the snake bite were fatal to my mother.

I was at the College again and someone came to tell me there was a call from Western Union and that it was something I should not worry about.

Although reassured, yet I was not so sure. How, I wondered, did they know it was nothing to worry about?

"Hello, this is Legson."

"I have your telegram here," he answered. "It's good," he continued, as if he also was worried.

NYAKAWONGA (mother's name) AND CHILDREN SEND THEIR GREETINGS. GOOD LUCK.

I sighed with relief. I still had a mother. I smiled at the other faces in the room and went out to telephone Mrs. Atwood that my mother apparently was well. But what about those strange dreams?

Mr. Atwood was building a garage. He gave me some instructions about using the power saw, how to put shingles together, and so on, and during the summer, especially in the morning when he would be at Washington State College in Bellingham, where he was finishing up his work for an M.A., I would try my hand at carpentry. When he returned, he would do most of the hammering and sawing, and I would do most of the watching.

At the end of the summer I was interviewed by Mr. Paul Friggens of the *Reader's Digest*. The absence of glaring or flashing lights, which I had begun to associate with any interview, made this one enjoyable and not so formal. He was staying at the President Hotel, and he came to the College in the morning or the Atwoods' in the evening. We took a walk down the road, our long shadows trailing behind us as the sun began to set beyond the hills far away in front of us. We climbed over my electric fence, after switching it off, of course, and watched the cows munching in the field.

CHAPTER 10

People and Places

WHEN school resumed I changed my major from physics to political science. Other than this, nothing important happened. Then suddenly, toward the end of January, a flood of letters began to arrive. The correspondence was so heavy that one day I found myself holding some eighty-five letters. I did not know what to do about answering them. They were in response to Mr. Friggens' article in the *Reader's Digest*.

Letters came in from many places. I remember one that amused me immensely. It came from a girl in West Germany with whom I had corresponded in 1956–57 while at Livingstonia. She wrote that she thought I was dead when she failed to hear from me for so long.

I sat down at the typewriter and answered as many of the letters as I could, and since some of them had money enclosed I was able to defray the postage expenses.

Miss Helmer was going to drive me to Seattle one Thursday afternoon. Television interview again. Bright lights again!

We arrived at the Olympic Hotel late in the afternoon and had the first of a series of interviews. That one was to be televised that evening. I went to dinner and failed to watch it. I started the next day by appearing on "Telescope," KING-TV. Then came a radio interview with KOMO, another radio interview with Associated Press, and lunch. I ended the day with a radio and television interview with KIRO. By the time we left for Mount Vernon, I was dog tired.

The number of letters mounted. Invitations to speak to different organizations in different places also mounted. I received such a letter from the Reverend Dr. W. O. Vaught in Little Rock. Of course I could not leave my studies and go on speaking tours, especially in faraway places such as Little Rock.

However, the coming summer found me relatively free. I did not go to summer school, and as a result I accepted three long-distance appointments. The first was in Sacramento, the second in Kansas City, Missouri, and the third in Little Rock.

In Sacramento I was to speak before a church group, and then to a Rotary Club the following day. One of the members of the club, Mr. Jackson Karns, was to come to Mount Vernon to pick me up in his private plane. In Kansas City I was to speak before the Rotary Club also, as a guest of Mr. Joe Gilbert. Here, Mr. Gilbert and Dr. Vaught in Little Rock—after I had notified Dr. Vaught that I had also accepted the invitation of Mr. Gilbert, which preceded the other by less than a week—had made arrangements between themselves for one group to pay my plane ticket to those places, and for the other group to pay for my ticket back to Mount Vernon.

It was June 7. Mr. Karns was due to arrive in Mount Vernon that afternoon and we would be taking off the following morning. I had my speeches all ready, one to deliver to the church group and the other to the club. Late in the afternoon Mr. Karns telephoned from the airfield in Mount Vernon to say that the weather forecast for the following morning was rather poor, that we had better leave that same afternoon and go to Yakima, where the forecast was more favorable. Would I remember to bring a light load? I took only my briefcase, in which I stuffed in a hurry two white shirts, two neckties, some philosophy books and writing papers and an extra pair of socks. Miss Helmer drove me to the airfield.

It was a four-seater plane. Mr. Karns' wife sat in the back seat. I sat in front beside Mr. Karns, the pilot and navigator. I could see the many instruments on the panel in front.

The motor began, the machine shook, and we moved toward the other end of the field. I had never been in a small plane before. There I was, sitting beside the pilot, where I had a good view of how planes are flown, and where I could see whatever happened to us. We turned around and stopped. The machine heaved, the engine made a piercing noise, and we rushed forward, forward. At first I thought we were going to overshoot the field, but a few seconds later the ground was fast receding below us. In a little while we were flying over the Cascade Range, and there, turning to me, Mr. Karns asked:

"Would you like to steer a little?"

Would I?

"Sure," I answered. For a few minutes I was steering, but really the plane was flying on automatic controls.

The following day, a few hours after leaving Yakima, we arrived in Sacramento, where I was the house guest of Mr. and Mrs. Norman Anderson. That afternoon Mrs. Anderson and a few other ladies drove me to the Capitol, where I had a most pleasant chat with Governor Pat Brown. I toured the city all the next day and then came the day when I was to deliver my first speech in the church.

"Slow down," my speech teacher used to remind me whenever I stood up to give an assigned speech lesson.

"Remember," Miss Helmer was telling me as she drove me to the airfield, "that these people have gone to a lot of expense so they can hear you. Speak slowly."

"You speak a little bit too fast," Mr. Karns said when we arrived in Sacramento. "Try to speak louder and slower, or some of the folks at the back will not understand you."

The church comprised two groups and I spoke to both of them. Standing in front of one of my biggest audiences, and wearing my one-year-old suit, I began speaking on missions and missionaries. At first I trembled and my nervousness showed in my voice. I decided it was because I was conscious of the way I spoke. All right, don't be conscious, but all the same, speak slow and a bit loud! I spoke slow and loud when I remembered the advice, now soft and fast when I forgot. From the response I got at the end, they had been able to understand me.

In the evening I gave another speech in another church, and I spent the following morning touring some points of interest in San Francisco. I went up to the Top of the Mark, across the Golden Gate Bridge, and on the cable cars. I came back to Sacramento to speak to the Rotary Club. In all those places they were kind enough to give me an honorarium, which was sent to my trust fund at Skagit. The next day I flew back to Mount Vernon. This time there were four of us in the plane, as the Karnses' son came along.

It so happened that I was scheduled to fly to Kansas City the following evening, and as soon as we got to Mount Vernon I was already getting ready for the other trip. But my ticket had not arrived. Early in the morning Miss Helmer telephoned Mr. Gilbert, who said that he hoped we would buy the ticket and that his group would refund the money when I got there. The College bought me the ticket, and taking my briefcase but with another set of clothes, I was on the bus for Seattle where I took the jet to Kansas City via Denver.

Late in the afternoon of the following day I was shaking hands with Mr. Gilbert, who had come to meet me. He drove me to my hotel, where I had a TV interview, and this done I went to his house for dinner. He and his family and guests all wondered what I was going to find in Little Rock. I had some ideas of my own, for I remembered the gentleman in Khartoum saying, "Have you ever heard of Little Rock?"

I delivered my speech the next day in a big room in the hotel where I was living. I was getting used to speaking before groups of people I did not know, and I discovered that the more calmly I spoke, the easier I found it to speak slow and loud. In the afternoon I took off for Little Rock.

At the airport a slender white gentleman walked toward me. I would have to be on my guard, I reminded myself.

"Mr. Kayira?" he asked, struggling with the pronunciation of my name.

"Yes," I confirmed.

"Welcome to Little Rock," he said. "I am Reverend Vaught."

I was in Little Rock now and I would see for myself what it was that made Little Rock so famous that I had heard of it long before I set foot in America.

"I'm sure you have heard of Little Rock," Dr. Vaught said as we drove into the city. "Well, here it is."

Yes, there it was. We stopped at his church, the Immanuel Baptist Church. It was in the downtown area. I saw many people, and they all seemed to mind their own business.

"There," he pointed at a school as we drove to his house from the church, "is where we had all those riots."

It was quite hot, and I was sipping a glass of iced tea in Dr. Vaught's house, engaged in an amicable discussion with his son, who was a graduate student at Yale University. Presently another gentleman was shown in, and introduced to me as Mr. Ralph Creger. Soon he and I entered into a lengthy discussion about the race problem in this country, and especially in Little Rock. I have to be on my guard, I reminded myself. I apologized that I did not have any firsthand knowledge of the problem and was unable to carry on any constructive discussion of it. I said that he should excuse me if I ended up doing most of the listening. He handed me a small book titled *This Is What We Found*, which he and his high-school-age son had written. I spent the best part of that evening reading the book in an attempt to familiarize myself with the problem as described by those who had witnessed the riots.

I would not go into the city on my own or unaccompanied, although I personally saw no reason why I should not. However, the next morning Dr. Vaught drove me to their press house for an interview. After the interview we drove to the shop of a gentleman whose name I am sorry to say I do not recall. On the way Dr. Vaught briefed me about him. He was, he said, a man who had been one of the most outspoken racists in Little Rock in 1959, but he had changed his ways and had "even joined the church."

"Yes, I was a racist," he told me as we sat in his shop. "I was against integration, but then I was told about the Lord, and I accepted Him. Now I have changed all my ways. It's all bad, that. . . ." He was getting excited with his story. He paused and looked at my shoes. He saw that they were old.

"Choose any pair you like here," he said, pointing at a row of shoes. "I really mean it."

I hesitated.

"I am not kidding," he said. "How about this one? Try it."

I tried it. The shoe was too big. I tried another one. It fitted. It belonged to a black pair with a pointed toe. He gave them to me!

I had a tour of the city, then I was driven to the home of another white family where they had a dinner party. The many people I met there were very friendly and they asked frankly what I thought about the race situation. I got so familiar with them that when it was time for me to deliver my speech on Sunday evening I did not feel as uncomfortable as I had thought I would. Everything was calm and orderly.

I flew back to Mount Vernon by way of Dallas and Los

Angeles. I arrived at Dallas Airport in the afternoon, and since it was going to be some hours before I left for Los Angeles, I thought I would go and have something to eat to pass the time. What a way to pass the time!

I proceeded to a big restaurant. A white lady was standing at the door and as I and several other people were about to enter, she asked me to stop. "This is it," I said to myself. "I may not be in Little Rock, but I am still in the South." I waited until the others were in. Then she asked:

"What do you want?"

Certainly this can't be the way you should welcome a customer, I thought. Be calm!

"I want to eat," I said.

"I'm sorry," she said with a funny drawl. "We don't have what you want to eat here."

"That's funny," I said. "How do you know you don't have what I want to eat before knowing what I want to eat?"

I feared we might get into an argument. We did not, for soon she conferred with a fellow worker, and the gentleman did not hesitate to let me in, only he arranged that I was given a room all to myself with a man of my color sent to serve me.

I was disappointed that I did not have enough time to see much of Los Angeles when I landed there, but with the little time I had at my disposal I managed to take a taxi downtown and around some points of interest.

Back in Washington I went to Wenatchee, where I was to work with the YMCA as a counselor at one of the camps. During the first two weeks in Wenatchee I was in charge of eight eight-year-old boys. This was probably one of the most difficult assignments I ever had—keeping a close eye on the boys, especially when we camped out for the night. One of my worries while camping out was that I could not cook very well, and certainly I could not expect much in the way of help from a boy eight years old. I did my best, and since they never complained, I have always assumed that they liked my cooking.

My most difficult problem was keeping the boys quiet when it was bedtime. I had to make sure they went to bed at their regular time, you know. I would tell them all sorts of bedtime stories, but I was absolutely warned against telling them any "scary stories." During the day, if we were not away on a trip, I taught them how to play soccer and, later on, archery. (They got their swimming lessons from other counselors.) I thought it amusing later when I failed Archery at Skagit. My problem was not that I did not know how to shoot a bow and arrow. Rather, it was that I shot too far. I stood some thirty yards away from the target, and my arrows would land something like a hundred yards beyond the target. Since the purpose of the course was to see how well and how often one could hit the bull's eye, naturally I failed the course.

During the next two weeks in Wenatchee I was assigned ten twelve-year-old boys, and with these I could feel more self-assured. We went out for two nights at a time, staying up on the mountain, in the forests, or beside some beautiful lakes. This time, in addition to teaching soccer and archery, I taught them how to shoot BB guns. I had to use my gumption here, because I had never shot a BB gun before.

I received a letter from Dr. K. E. Whickam, of Louisiana, in which she asked if I would attend a beauty convention in Cleveland that summer. Of course, I would attend the convention as an observer and not as a participant. All expenses would be paid. A beauty convention! Well, that's where all the beautiful ladies would be. I gratefully accepted.

I was in Seattle talking with one of the "Three Stooges" who was to drive me to the airport. He said that O'Hare International Airport was one of the world's busiest airports, with about one hundred and thirty-five planes landing and taking off each minute. I agreed with the first part of the statement, but I was rather skeptical of the figure. I could hardly believe that the world had so many planes that it could keep feeding Chicago with a hundred and thirty-five each minute. But I was going to be practical. Since I was going to make a quick stop at O'Hare to change planes to Cleveland, I could count the planes.

I landed there early the next morning. Without losing any time, I went up on the deck to count the planes that arrived and left. I counted quite a few, but not a hundred and thirty-five. In an effort to get a better average, I kept on counting planes and, as it were, I even counted my plane to Cleveland. Suddenly I realized that I had been on the deck too long. But it was worth it, for nothing else fascinates me more than watching helicopters and jets. I would look with the greatest admiration and amazement at the big jets speeding on the runway, thrusting into the air with the black smoke rushing out behind them and their great noise almost deafening me. After a few minutes I forgot all about counting them, but I could never cease marveling at them.

The invitation to Cleveland was unique in one respect. I was not asked to give a speech but simply to attend the beauty contest, which was sponsored by the National Institute of Cosmetics. Nobody met me at the airport and I had to depend upon the bus driver to direct me to the Pick-Carter Hotel, where I was to stay, and where the contesting beauties were also staying.

There were girls, girls, girls everywhere in the lounge when I entered. I showed my letter to the man at the desk—it had been sent to me by the hotel before I left Wenatchee—and he immediately showed me to my room. I was only interested in coming down to meet as many of the girls as possible, but when I stared at my image in the mirror, I was not so sure. My hair was long because I seldom cut it, and being uncombed as it was that afternoon, it made me appear strange to myself. I hurriedly combed it, and when I began changing my clothes I laughed when I discovered that I was still wearing my pajamas under my suit. The reason for this unusual manner of dressing was quite simple. After I had packed my things when I was leaving Washington I had discovered that I had not packed my pajamas. Not wishing to open my bag again, I had decided to wear them under the suit.

I was in Cleveland for four days, chatting with the beauties. They numbered in the hundreds. On the final day, there was a dinner party where two winners were announced for some part of the general contest. I think it was for hair-do. The two winners were given round-trip tickets to Paris.

After the two happy girls had got over the initial shock and excitement at winning such a grand prize for their skills in beautifying themselves, Dr. Whickam, who was president of the Institute, rose to speak. First she read a message from President Kennedy, and then went on to say:

"Now we have another person here at the head table who will also receive a prize, a scholarship."

I looked at the pretty ladies on my left, then at those on my right, and back at those in front of the head table. There were a few men in the audience, among them a reporter who had interviewed me earlier in the day.

"The person who is to receive the scholarship didn't take part in the contest," she said, "but we know that he . . ."

He? My body trembled. Who else at the head table would be described as "he"? Dr. Whickam talked for some time about me and then asked me to stand. The pretty girls I had come all the way from Washington to see clapped their hands. I stood up shyly; felt embarrassed and most humble that I, with the hair, whose cutting was several months overdue, should sit next to the girls whose very hair had enabled them to win grand prizes.

Dr. Whickam put her hand on my shoulder and said:

"We are giving him a scholarship of one thousand dollars."

One thousand dollars! What had I done to deserve it? My lips quivered like a reed in a stream. I gasped a few words, but I was unable to find any meaning in them. I stood stiff and unbelieving, staring at the check, which was to be sent to the trust fund. I said, "Thank you." Those were the only words I knew to say, the only words I had said to the people in Mount Vernon, and the only words I could offer to those people and to all their fellow countrymen.

"Thank you," I repeated.

CHAPTER 11

I Will Keep on Trying

Isn't it a beautiful coincidence that I should be writing this portion of the book under the roof of my mother's house? Oh no, I am not dreaming. I am really here.

I look to the east and I see a hill, a big one. I look to the west and I see another big hill. Neither looks any taller or shorter than when I left it almost six years ago. There was a time when I scaled their heights and never dreamed I would not see them for as long as six years. These hills were part of my life and wherever I went, I would point to them and say, "There is my home."

I look to the north, then to the south, and all I see is a slender valley whose entire length is cut in two by the Didimu River. It was in this valley one harvesting season many years ago, God knows how many years ago, I was born. Had fate been unkind to me at that time, it was this same river that would have swallowed me, leaving only a memory in the mind of my mother and a few who saw the big, fat baby later to be called Didimu.

My mother is still here. I know it because I have been reunited with her. In fact, I am looking at her now as I write this. She is still young-looking and still unable to comprehend the fact that America is considerably more than five days away on foot but only about a day by jet.

I surprised her. She did not know I was coming on that particular day. I had written to say that I expected to come home for the summer, but I never gave her the exact day. I realized that she would have been very excited had I been able to tell her the exact day of my arrival. (Excitement was part and parcel of my entire homecoming.) But I also realized that if I told her, she would spend the whole day waiting anxiously for her prodigal. If for some unforeseen reason I failed to show up on that particular day, even if it were possible that I should show up the very next day, I feared I would find her in a miserable mood.

I flew to Blantyre from Seattle in the company of Mr. Lane Smith, a reporter for the Seattle *Times*, who, among other things, was to cover Nyasaland's Independence celebrations. We traveled by Land Rover from Blantyre to Mpale, my village, arriving here a little before noon on a sunny Saturday. My mother and my sister were sitting in front of the house. They have changed houses since I left, and if it were not for the help of an old friend who hitchhiked a ride with us, Mr. Smith and I would have been temporarily lost. The Land Rover pulled in a few yards from where they were sitting. I daresay they were startled, because few cars, if any, had ever stopped here.

I jumped out, and no sooner had I done so than my mother recognized me. Quick as a wink the neighbors learned I had come. Already Mr. Smith was getting the credit for bringing me home!

My brother and my sister are both here. They are pupils at one of the schools I attended myself. They were not able to recognize me any more than I could recognize them. They have grown up. My brother seems very quiet, very reserved. He stammers when he speaks, and he tells me he began stammering less than two years ago.

I have been here in my old home for several days now and I am now convinced that I am not dreaming. I have met again a good many of the people who lived here when I also lived here. Some of them, of course, have left us for the next world. Some are already stooping down when they walk by reason of the heavy weight of age. Those who were born after I left do not know me and they still run away from me. Most of the people say that I have changed, that I do not look as I did before. I say they have changed too, that the whole village has changed. Could it be that we all have changed? Yet I would have recognized my mother anywhere, and she was able to recognize me in no time at all.

However, my village looks very different, and for a time I was almost convinced that nobody understood me, although I spoke in my own language—theirs too, by the way.

Now that I am sitting here, almost fully reunited with my beginnings, I look back to that October morning almost six years ago. "You are mad, you are really mad," Kaliyokha had said. He is still here and he still thinks I am mad. I may have had a wild dream then, but even with that wild dream I could hardly have believed I would get where I was going and that one day I would fly back home for a holiday. I remember my mother spitting in my face, giving me her short but classic advice.

"God is powerful," one woman cried when she came to embrace me that Saturday morning I arrived in Mpale. "He has brought our child home!"

God is powerful, that we know. I am wondering, though, what would have become of me if I had not left or if I had abandoned my plans on the way and given up. Well, I do not know because I did not give up. Possibly I would be working somewhere in the country and raising a family.

During the short period since I have been home I have visited most of my relatives and old friends, even those who live a considerable distance from my village. I have been to see the family of our ex-family doctor. I am told that the doctor himself was not able to survive the bite of a black mamba.

I have already visited my old school, Livingstonia. It has changed too to some extent but it still gives one the feeling and the urge for scholarship. The man who built it must

have had monumental plans for it. I have already seen several
new primary schools. In all these schools I have seen the
happy pupils, whose faces beam at one with smiles of appreciation of their opportunities, and encouragement of their
time. They may not have the same opportunities as their
American counterparts, but they are accepting all that their
country can possibly give them.

These pupils seem to take their work seriously. It is a matter of competition, especially for those who have their hearts
set on some college or university. They *must* get there. For
them this is no longer a world of complacency as it may
have been for their fathers. They know that the future of
their country lies in their hands. In the old days one went to
school to learn how to read and write and one survived
pretty well. These young people realize now that for them
and their country to survive, they will need more than just
learning how to read and write. Their philosophy is not:
"Ask and you shall receive." Rather it is: "Labor and you
shall gain."

How difficult is it to get an American scholarship? This
is the question I have been asked many times by these young
people. I do not know what the answer is. I cannot answer
for any country. I cannot answer for any university, even
for my own University of Washington. I do not know, but
like my questioners I would wish it were easier.

Is it possible for one from here to enter a secondary school
in America? This is another question that they have often
asked me. I should think so. I know of some high schools that
have exchange programs with other countries. I should think
this is one of the most constructive ways of cultivating
friendship between or among nations. In some cases this exchange should prove better than if it were done on a college
level. Why do I think so? Well, I believe that misunderstanding often breeds conflict, and that if countries encouraged
the exchange of their young people to study in other countries, even for a short time and at a time when they have not

yet acquired lifelong traditional ideas, often wrong ideas, of other cultures, maybe something could be done toward clearing this cloud of misunderstanding that prevails over us all.

As I sit here, I look back at the near past, when I began writing this book. Certainly it never occurred to me that I would write part of it in my homeland. I laugh now, but I also realize that there was a time when I wept. At that time, or to be more correct, at those times, I never thought I would sit down and write a book at all.

I started to write for two reasons. I have mentioned that I used to get many invitations to speak. As a full-time student, I could hardly accept all these engagements or even half of them. I had to disappoint many groups and organizations by turning down their invitations. And some of these had seen to it that I got my transportation from Khartoum to Skagit Valley College. It was suggested that I write down my experiences in a page or two and pass them on to the groups who asked me to speak. Being unable to limit my memories to two pages, I found myself dividing the whole thing into sections, which roughly corresponded to the present chapters.

"Your language is too formal," my English professor at the University of Washington said. "Reading your report is just like reading a legal document."

I had transferred to the big University of Washington in Seattle then. Since I had never done very well in any English course at Skagit, I decided to enroll in another English course at the University. Now my professor was saying that my language was too formal. I planned to write a rebuff and I was going to write it on something I knew. So I took my pen and tried to polish up what I had already written at Skagit, deleting some words that I thought sounded formal, and putting in those I thought less formal, even informal. This was the second act that led to the writing of this book. First I had wanted to save time, and second, I decided to use it as a practice exercise for my English course.

During my first summer in Seattle, I stayed with Dr. and Mrs. F. J. Lane. Mrs. Lane read the papers (for now they were many), and wondered what I could do with them. As far as I was concerned, I assured her, there was nothing I could do with them except to send them to the dust bin where they belonged.

"No, you don't!" she said.

She suggested that I expand them and then see what I could do with them. Mrs. Rose Norwalk, who lived in the same neighborhood, also read the papers. The two ladies would not let me throw them away. I began expanding them until they became this book.

I am writing all this because I am reviewing all of it in my mind as I sit here. It looks as if I have just waked up from a long sleep with a long dream that took me to far distant lands, to the very edge of the earth. I am thinking of my homes in Mount Vernon and in Seattle, as well as my original home here where I am now. Indeed, I can say that I feel like I am a child of two nations, appreciating two cultures, one that I was born to and the other that was once foreign to me, but which is now becoming familiar. I know that I have almost failed to make a perfect adjustment in the former culture, but I also know that this is an error not to be repeated again.

Most people, including my mother, are surprised to learn that I have not come back here for good, that I shall be here for three months only.

"What is it that you are looking for?" they ask me.

"See so-and-so," my mother says. "He is younger than you are, but he is already working."

"You must marry now," the big men of the village tell me. "Settle down."

There is nothing I am looking for, I try to tell them. Staying at home now would not make any more sense than if I had stayed home six years ago. Surely I have been to America, and although this alone would give me a different outlook, my purpose for going there was to obtain an education. I have not yet graduated from my university. I have to comfort my mother by assuring her that this goal will be attained before the end of a year. After that, there will be a year or two of postgraduate work. At any rate, I should be back here within three years.

CHAPTER 12

A Salute to Malawi

T HE soldiers who had been parading came to a stop and stood at attention. They were in the grounds of the huge Central Stadium of Blantyre-Limbe.

Thousands of spectators moved on their seats and exchanged whispers with their neighbors, then there was silence again. Only the sound of the clock could be heard, slowly ticking toward midnight and at the same time building up impatience and anxiety in the souls of the spectators.

"God bless our gracious Queen . . ." The serious band played the noble anthem. Thousands were standing. Then there was a short period of darkness as the lights in the stadium were turned off, then light again. The proud Union Jack had finally come down and the world's newest flag, bearing the colors of black, red, and green, had unfurled and was now flying. Then the world's newest anthem, "O God Bless Our Land of Malawi," was played:

> O God bless our land of Malawi,
> Keep it a land of peace,
> Put down each and every enemy,
> Hunger, disease, envy.
> Join together all our hearts as one,
> That we be free from fear.
> Bless our leader, each and everyone,
> And Mother Malawi.

There was an outburst of cheers and singing. A new nation had been born and they called it Malawi.

How touching it is to witness one's country's triumph of becoming free. How beautiful it is! It gives one a feeling of pride and of achievement. It makes one proud, as one's parents are proud of their baby, and proud of one's time and generation.

Future generations of Malawi will inherit independence and freedom. They will not have the same feelings for it as the Malawians of this day. They will probably take it for granted. Those today who have worked hard for it know that it is only by hard work that this independence will survive.

One may look at the past, the near past, in the history of Nyasaland, now Malawi. It has not been much longer than seventy-three years that the Union Jack has flown over this land, and during this time the people have struggled and advanced to independence. Now the land is free and so are its people.

We know that with the spirit that has directed this country and its people in the past, the independence of this country can be assured. My people know how they fought for freedom, how many people lost their lives so others could be free. They know that if we should lose this independence, the next struggle for it could be more difficult, more ruthless, and might be useless.

On July 6, 1964, I wrote for the Seattle *Times:*

"Nine score and eight years ago, a few men later to be the prideful forefathers of one of the greatest nations ever to be created by the Lord, took one of the boldest steps in the history of mankind: They decided to declare themselves free and independent of the mighty Empire of Britain.

"They were few, but very dedicated. They were alone, but trusting in the great powers of their Maker.

"They may have been ridiculed and laughed at; they may have doubted their own decision, but they held on to it fast and strong, and what was then a desire of the few came, in their future generations, to be a desire of the millions.

"Nine score and eight years later, a new nation has been born, created and founded by one Dr. H. Kamuzu Banda and freed, as it were, from the same grand Empire.

"Were the Lord to instruct that the Americans of that day should return to America today, how proud would they be to find that the little nation they founded is now far beyond what their petty imaginations could then conceive!

"Now, it is Malawi that takes the same bold step. She has decided to declare herself free and independent.

"There may be some who are laughing at Malawi now; there may be some who are waiting to see what will happen to her, but she is holding on to her decision.

"In the streets, on the trails, in the towns, in the villages, hundreds upon hundreds of Malawians sing and cheer and talk of the Grand Day. . . .

"This is their nation. They have helped found it, and if the Lord were to instruct that they should return to their nation, nine score and eight years from now, how proud they would be on that day to find that the nation they founded was still striving and surviving all odds!"

A salute to you, Malawi, and godspeed. We have just begun to try.